1997

The Management of International Joint Ventures

Over the past two decades there has been a substantial increase in the formation of international joint ventures. For many firms, JVs have become the mainstay of competitive strategy. This book examines various IJV management issues, with a particular focus on collaboration and organizational learning. A primary objective in the book is to develop some clear linkages between organizational learning concepts and learning through IJVs. To provide a realistic perspective of IJV management and to develop managerial implications, examples drawn from multiple sources of data are utilized throughout the book. The examples and comment from managers illustrate many of the concepts discussed and anchor the research in managerial practice.

The book begins with an overview of JV characteristics, performance and control for a sample of Japanese–North American JVs. It then shifts to a detailed examination of learning through collaboration. The focus is on how JV partners exploit and lever alliance knowledge. Organizational dimensions shaping the learning process are considered and some of the more controversial areas in organizational learning are examined as the basis for developing a multi-level learning framework. The final issue considered is the relationship between learning, collaborative knowledge and IJV stability.

Andrew Inkpen is Assistant Professor of Management at Thunderbird, the American Graduate School of International Management. He previously held faculty positions at Temple University and the National University of Singapore. His research focuses on international strategic management, with an emphasis on the management of international alliances. His research has appeared in various journals, including the *Strategic Management Journal, Journal of International Business Studies* and *Long Range Planning*.

International Business Series
Academic Editor: Alan M. Rugman,
University of Toronto

The Management of International Joint Ventures

An Organizational Learning Perspective

Andrew Inkpen

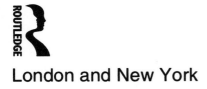

London and New York

First published 1995
by Routledge
11 New Fetter Lane, London EC4P 4EE

Simultaneously published in the USA and Canada
by Routledge
29 West 35th Street, new york, NY 10001

Typeset in Times by LaserScript Ltd. Mitcham, Surrey
Printed and bound in Great Britain by
Mackays of Chatham PLC, Chatham, Kent

British Library Cataloguing in Publication Data
A catalogue record for this book is available from the British Library

Library of Congress Cataloguing in Publication Data
A catalogue record for this book has been requested

ISBN 0–415–11706–2

Contents

Illustrations

Acknowledgements

Helpful comments have been provided by numerous colleagues. In particular, the book has benefited from the support of Paul Beamish, Mary Crossan, Peter Killing and Rod White of the Western Business School and Allen Morrison of Thunderbird, The American Graduate School of International Management. The contributions of Harry Lane, Shige Makino, Jim Rush and Pat Woodcock are also acknowledged. I am also grateful for the time and valuable information provided by the managers who shared their JV experiences with me. This research would not have been possible without their cooperation. Finally, I would like to acknowledge the excellent editorial assistance and overall support received from my wife, Patricia Seary.

This book would not have been possible without the financial support provided by the Carnegie Bosch Institute for Applied Studies in International Management, based at Carnegie Mellon University and the Centre for International Business Studies, based at the Western Business School of the University of Western Ontario.

Earlier versions of Chapters 2, 7 and 9 were originally published as follows. An earlier version of Chapter 2 appeared as 'The characteristics and performance of Japanese–North American joint ventures in North America' in *Advances in International Comparative Management* 9, 1994. Chapter 7 appeared as 'Believing is seeing: joint ventures and organization learning' in *Journal of Management Studies*, September, 1995. Chapter 9 appeared as 'Keeping international joint ventures stable and profitable' in *Long Range Planning*, June 1995.

Chapter 1

Introduction

The continued growth in the formation of alliances and joint ventures (JVs) has lead to speculation that today's notion of global firms will be superseded by networks of strategic alliances among firms spanning many different industries and countries. One of the driving forces behind the increased use of strategic alliances is the realization by many firms that self-sufficiency is becoming increasingly difficult in an international business environment that demands both strategic focus and flexibility. Alliances provide the opportunity for firms to leverage their strengths with the help of partners.

This book focuses on the management of equity JVs, one of the most common forms of international alliances. For this book, a JV is defined as a means of performing activities in combination with one or more firms instead of autonomously. A JV occurs when two or more legally distinct firms (the parents) pool a portion of their resources within a jointly owned legal organization. This definition excludes other forms of cooperative agreements such as licensing, distribution and supply agreements, research and development partnerships, or technical assistance and management contracts.

Using multiple sources of field-based data, the book examines various JV management issues, with a particular focus on collaboration and organizational learning. A primary objective in the book is to develop some clear linkages between organizational learning concepts and learning through JVs. To provide a realistic perspective of IJV management and to develop managerial implications, examples drawn from in-depth interviews are utilized throughout the book. The examples and comments from managers illustrate many of the concepts discussed and anchor the research in managerial practice.

THE EMPIRICAL BASE

Over the past decade there has been a wave of Japanese investment in the North American automotive industry, both at the assembler and supplier levels. Much of the Japanese investment has involved JVs between Japanese and North American firms. A multi-stage project examining North American–Japanese JVs provides the primary empirical base for this book. The research stages include:

1   an initial field survey of 40 North American–Japanese JVs;
2   a longitudinal case study involving a subset of the JVs examined in the initial study (see the Appendix for a detailed discussion of the research methodology).

The Japanese–North American JVs provided an interesting data source because for many of the US firms, JV involvement represented the first close US-based relationship with both a Japanese partner and a Japanese customer. For many of the Japanese firms, a JV was the first significant investment outside Japan. In collecting the data and interacting with JV managers, it was possible to observe firms struggling with many of the strategic and operational problems inherent in IJV management.

JVs AND ORGANIZATIONAL LEARNING

A variety of strategic objectives has been suggested to explain firms' motives for the formation of JVs (Beamish and Banks 1987; Contractor and Lorange 1988; Hennart 1988; Porter and Fuller 1986). The objectives include the reduction of risk, economies of scale, access to technology or markets, and the search for legitimacy. In much of the JV literature, the focus has been on firms' mutual desire to cooperate as the basis for JV formation. This focus emphasizes the performance of the JV task and the benefits of pooling resources and skills for cooperative results.

After discussing JV characteristics and several performance issues, the focus of the book shifts to a detailed examination of learning through collaboration. The focus is on how JV partners exploit and leverage alliance knowledge. Viewing JVs as learning opportunities provides an alternative to mutual JV value creation. JVs can provide firms with access to the embedded knowledge of other organizations. This access creates the potential for firms to internalize partner skills and capabilities. In an alliance, two or more organizations are brought together because of their complementarity and their differences. The differences in partner skill areas are the fuel for learning. Whether or not the differences are identified and internalized determines whether learning occurs. An important conclusion from this research is that while organizations often talk in glowing terms about their alliances' learning potential, learning is a difficult, frustrating, and often misunderstood process.

STRUCTURE OF THE BOOK

The initial chapters deal with some fundamental JV issues and provide a contextual overview of the organizations examined in the book. Chapter 2 draws on survey data to examine characteristics of the Japanese–North American JVs. After examining the JVs in terms of ownership, formation objectives, initiation, and management style, the issue of JV performance is considered. The concluding section raises some issues associated with JV termination and JVs as a viable organizational form.

Chapter 3 considers the implications for North American firms gaining temporary, and perhaps even permanent access to Japanese networks through the formation of JVs with Japanese firms. The chapter first provides an overview of Japanese corporate networks, emphasizing corporate relationships in the automotive industry. The transfer of Japanese networks to North America is then considered as the basis for examining problems US managers have encountered when confronted with the ambiguity and uncertainty of Japanese networks.

Chapter 4 examines an important theme in the literature on IJVs – the relationship between JV control and performance. The main argument in the chapter is that control over JV activities creates a dependency perspective and, therefore, a lack of bargaining power in a particular area is potentially a key factor in the evaluation of JV performance. Three different conceptualizations of the control–performance relationship are examined using both the survey data and an additional sample of Japanese JVs.

Chapter 5 shifts the focus to the organizational learning issue. Given the premise that IJVs create learning opportunities for the venture partners, this chapter explores the conceptual background associated with learning and collaboration.

Chapter 6 begins with a discussion of the learning experience of the American JV parents and their efforts to exploit JV learning opportunities. The chapter then empirically examines organizational dimensions that can shape the learning experience. The dimensions examined are:

1 learning capacity;
2 parent experience;
3 partner interactions.

Chapter 7 builds on the earlier conceptual discussion. Some of the more controversial areas in the organizational learning literature are examined as the basis for developing a multi-level learning framework. The framework provides the underpinnings for the argument that an existing set of managerial beliefs can constrain the learning process. Applying the framework to the JV context provides insights into why firms with explicit learning objectives struggled to capitalize on their JV learning opportunities.

Chapter 8 provides seven case vignettes dealing with JV management. The vignettes provide some 'thick' description of JV issues such as JV learning potential, JV failure, performance and learning, and collaborative knowledge management.

Chapter 9 examines the relationship between learning, collaborative knowledge, and IJV stability. If IJVs are inherently unstable organizational forms, as researchers and managers have suggested, why do some ventures survive and prosper for many years? This chapter argues that foreign partner knowledge of the local economic, political, and cultural environments is a critical factor in the stability of IJVs. When the foreign partner is no longer satisfied with access to local knowledge and seeks to acquire this knowledge, the probability of JV instability increases substantially. This chapter suggests that if managers are aware of the factors influencing JV stability, they may be able to prevent or control for premature changes in partner relationships.

Finally, the concluding chapter examines the organizational learning and IJV findings from two theoretical perspectives: resource-based theories of strategy and transaction costs.

Chapter 2

Japanese JVs

Characteristics and performance

This chapter draws on the survey data to examine the characteristics of the Japanese–North American JVs.[1] After examining the JVs in terms of ownership, formation objectives, initiation, and management style, the issue of JV performance is considered. The concluding section raises some issues associated with JV termination and JVs as a viable organizational form.

THE AUTOMOTIVE INDUSTRY

Five key trends characterized the automotive supply industry of the late 1980s. One, the assemblers were increasing their outsourcing of parts through the establishment of multi-tiered supplier arrangements. First-tier suppliers deal directly with the assemblers, the second-tier suppliers manage a third tier, and so on. Two, automakers were pushing their suppliers toward just-in-time delivery systems and increased investment in design and engineering capabilities. Three, mergers were becoming prevalent in the supplier sector, largely because of heavy demands for research and development, new equipment, and employee training. Four, suppliers were moving away from their traditional focus on home markets toward foreign investment. During the 1980s, more than 250 Japan-based supplier firms established operations in North America and most arrived in the 1987–88 period. Finally, the movement of the Japanese transplants into North America established an important new customer sector for North America-based suppliers.

By the early 1990s and mirroring the situation with automaking capacity, excess capacity at the supplier level was becoming a reality. With the US automakers under pressure from the Japanese companies, North American suppliers found their traditional customer base shrinking. The overcapacity and competition from foreign-based component suppliers created increasingly difficult conditions for North American automotive suppliers. These conditions were forcing North American suppliers to adapt to a very different competitive environment. A 1989 statement by a senior manager in a US component supplier reflects the new environment:

> The next five years are going to be horrible. With the new Japanese companies coming in, with peripheral capacity, and with component integration and the car companies all chasing the same market . . . a lot of suppliers are going to fall out.

> (Smith 1989: 37)

It was against the background of a changing automotive industry and the recent wave of Japanese–American supplier JVs that the JV survey was carried out.

JV CHARACTERISTICS

All the JVs studied were suppliers to the automotive industry and only one had less than 50 per cent of its sales to automotive customers. Most were direct suppliers to the automotive assemblers (i.e. tier one suppliers; see Table 2.1 for a summary of JV characteristics). Three-quarters of the ventures were manufacturers of parts and components while the remainder produced materials such as paint, steel, glass, and chemicals. In 27 cases, the JV products were functionally similar to existing American parent products. In the other 13 cases, the JV represented a product diversification for the American parent. The mean number of employees was 206 and 15 JVs had between 150 and 300 employees.

The American JV parents were almost evenly divided between single business firms and divisions of diversified firms. There were 22 single business parents and 18 diversified parents in the sample. In all but two cases, the JVs were startup or greenfield organizations. A JV was classified as a greenfield venture if an organization was created where none existed before. One of the non-greenfield ventures was formed when the American parent spun off a small downstream operation. In the other non-greenfield case, the American partner contributed an existing plant and domestic customer product line to the JV. The product line was subsequently expanded and a transplant customer base developed through the efforts of the Japanese partner.

Most JVs were comprised of single plants geographically separated from the American parents' facilities and, generally, new plants and

Table 2.1 JV characteristics

Characteristics	Number of cases	Per cent	Characteristics	Number of cases	Per cent
American partner equity (%)			**Number of years operational**		
20-30	4	10.0	1	2	5.0
31-40	5	12.5	2	5	12.5
41-48	3	7.5	3	14	35.0
49	3	7.5	4	12	30.0
50	17	42.5	5	5	12.5
51	4	10.0	6	2	5.0
60	4	10.0	——	——	——
JV customers		Tiers supplied (%)			
Tier 1	33	82.5	Single transplant	11	27.5
Tier 2	4	10.0	Multiple transplants	13	32.5
Tier 1 and Tier 2	3	7.5	US assemblers and transplants	11	27.5
			US assemblers	5	12.5

equipment were built or acquired specifically for the JVs. In four cases, the JVs acquired existing, unused plants from their American partners. In two cases, the JVs had separate production lines but leased space within existing American partner facilities, and in one case, the JV used American partner production lines exclusively (although a new plant was planned). In the fourth case, the JV bought land from the American partner and constructed a new plant on the site of an old plant. In several additional cases, the JVs began operations using American partner facilities and constructed new plants several years later.

Formation objectives

The cases were classified according to the American partner's motive in forming the JV. In making this classification, it was recognized that JV parents often are motivated by multiple factors in forming JVs. Thus, the motive represents the American partner's primary motivating factor.

The primary motive for 29 American partners was access to the transplant market. All but five JVs were transplant suppliers and 11 supplied a single transplant (Table 2.1). The prevalent opinion of managers involved with transplant customers was that American firm access to the transplant market would not have been possible without a Japanese connection. A Japanese JV partner was viewed as the most effective and timely means of acquiring the connection that would enable the American firms to become transplant suppliers. Within the American partner firms there was a strong belief that the Japanese transplants wanted to deal with Japanese suppliers and were willing to sacrifice the locational experience of American suppliers and even the potentially lower costs of American suppliers.[2]

Nine non-transplant access ventures were classified as technology oriented. Four American firms sought access to manufacturing technology and the capital necessary to implement the technology. In five cases, the primary motive was access to technology that would allow the American partner to broaden its product line and give the Japanese partner entry to the North American market. As an American parent executive commented, 'We had the market access through our own plants and the administration talent to run the business. We did not have the manufacturing expertise.'

The remaining two non-transplant access ventures involved risk-sharing and legitimacy. In the risk-sharing case, the two partners wished to enter the North American automotive market with a product both firms manufactured outside North America. The JV allowed the partners to combine forces and share the risk of entering a new market. In the legitimacy case, the formation of the JV was motivated by the desire of the American partner to collaborate with a Japanese firm because 'everyone else was doing it'. This motive is called legitimacy because the American partner was motivated to appear in agreement with the prevailing norms in the automotive industry. Several managers indicated that forming a JV with a Japanese partner was a very 'fashionable' thing to do during the period 1985–90.

Broadly speaking, all of the JVs were formed to strengthen an existing business. With the size of existing domestic markets stable or declining, a JV could compensate the American partners by providing relatively quick access to a new customer or product market. Consequently, many of the ventures were defensive and associated with an American parent attitude of 'we better form a JV before it is too late'.

While product and customer market motives provided a specific and often short-term objective for American firms, two less tangible objectives were also important. The first was a learning objective. Many of the American parent firms, struggling to compete in an industry in transition, saw their JVs as a point of leverage for the development of new skills and capabilities. The second was a desire to internationalize and move beyond domestic markets. As a JV manager explained:

> The JVs were formed because we felt we [the American partner] had to have a greater international presence in an industry that was rapidly becoming more international in scope. The American partner wanted to be a supplier with a 'window to the world'; the JV helps give us that window. Access to the transplant market may have provided an initial short-term objective for the formation of the JVs and it may have brought the firms together. However, our longer term objective is to become a world leader.

The manager went on to contend that alliances were critical to an international strategy and that the Japanese were much better at using alliances than North American firms. Another manager echoed those comments:

> We wanted to establish a global connection in the automotive supply industry. The JV is one step toward becoming a more international player in the automotive industry. We are now investigating alliances in Europe. The OEMs [assemblers] are getting closer to having common products across regions (i.e. North America and Europe). For a supplier it would be advantageous to be capable of supplying the same part in different parts of the world.

A common theme expressed by many managers was that gaining access to the transplant market provided the American firm with their first step toward becoming more international. The American firms usually recognized that the automotive industry was changing rapidly and wanted to participate in that change. Unfortunately, the objectives of transplant access and internationalization often took precedence over economic reasons for forming an alliance. Several managers indicated that 'faith' drove the JV formation process; both the American and Japanese firms entered the JV with little more than faith in each other. In these cases, neither partner communicated its objectives and little effort was made to establish financial objectives. Not surprisingly, many JVs subsequently experienced problems because of the lack of communication during the formation process.

Ownership

The predominant ownership relationship was equal partner equity (Table 2.1). In seven cases, equity had changed since the JV formation and in three of the seven cases, the Japanese partner had acquired the interest of its American partner. In the other four cases, the Japanese partner had significantly increased its equity position. In five additional cases, informants indicated a high probability that the Japanese partner would buy out their American partner. Thus, there were 12 cases in total where the Japanese partner increased or probably would increase its equity position in the JV. There was only one case in which the American partner increased its equity position.

The data suggest that JV ownership was associated with the type of JV customer. Eleven JVs were associated with a single transplant customer. Of these 11, seven were majority controlled by the Japanese partner. No ventures with a single transplant customer JV were American partner majority owned.

In the single transplant customer cases, Japanese partners were usually part of supplier groups in Japan. As part of a supplier group, the Japanese partners would normally be influenced by the expectations of the Japanese assemblers.[3] As several managers indicated, the expectations often revolved around JV ownership. The Japanese partner was often expected to have a controlling interest in the JV. In addition, the JV may have been expected to have only one customer.

The influence of the Japanese customers in partner selection and JV structure represents an important example of the type of leverage that Japanese customers can exert over their suppliers.[4] Many American managers, exposed for the first time to the Japanese system of supplier-manufacturer relationships, expressed concern about the leverage and unrelenting pressure from Japanese customers. One manager indicated that the Japanese use the expression 'squeezing a dry towel' to refer to a customer's relationship with its suppliers.

Chapter 3 considers in detail the relationship between Japanese suppliers and automakers. Briefly, if the Japanese suppliers had refused to follow their Japanese automaker customers to North America, they would have risked damaging the intricate network of implicit trading agreements that exists in Japan between suppliers and manufacturers. The Japanese automakers played a role in JV formation decisions because using JV suppliers may have helped alleviate some of the political concerns about 'screwdriver'[5] auto plants in the United States (Womack 1988). Thus, for many Japanese suppliers, a primary consideration in both the decision to invest in North America and the choice of the JV mode was the desire to maintain an existing supplier–manufacturer relationship.

JV initiation

American partners initiated about the same number of JVs as Japanese partners. For one-third of the JVs there was no clear initiator.[6] Ten of the cases without an initiator involved prior partner relationships, generally involving technology sharing and licensing agreements that began in the 1960s with the American firm transferring technology to Japan. Over the years, the agreements often evolved into two-way technology sharing arrangements. In several cases, technology sharing agreements resulted in the American and Japanese firms agreeing not to compete with each other in their home markets. These non-competition agreements provided the impetus for the formation of several JVs. The Japanese partner could not enter North America without breaking the agreement with its American partner and the American partner wanted access to the growing transplant market.

Not surprisingly, there was a relationship between initiation and ownership. Where there was a clear initiator, there was a trend toward that partner having majority control. Where there was no initiator, equal ownership was more common. The results also indicated a relationship between JV experience and initiation. When the American partner lacked JV experience, the JVs tended to be initiated by the Japanese partner or by both partners. There was only one case in which the American partner had no JV experience and initiated the JV.

Management style

The JVs were classified according to the predominant management style in the JV. Three classifications were used: Japanese, American, and hybrid. The hybrid style represents a mix of both Japanese and American management styles. The classification was based on various factors, including:

- the management structure in the JV;
- the number of senior American and Japanese JV managers;
- the JV customers;
- the visible aspects of the JV: uniforms, office layout.

The three styles are illustrated by short case examples. The first case is classified as a Japanese management style JV. This JV was formed to supply components to one of the transplants. The Japanese partner belonged to a Japanese supplier group and was 'encouraged' to locate in North America. The JV had only one customer and the Japanese partner was majority owner of the JV. The management team nominated by the Japanese partner included the president, the vice president administration, and vice president manufacturing. These managers were appointed for two-year terms in the JV. At the end of the two-year term the managers were repatriated to Japan. The American parent provided the executive vice president and personnel manager. There were no explicit plans to rotate these managers back to the American parent.

The manufacturing line and the products manufactured by the JV were copied from Japan. Personnel practices were based on the Japanese model: for example, all employees wore the same uniform; all workers were on salary; the plant was union-free; and monthly meetings were held with all employees to review issues like quality performance. The JV offices utilized an open office concept and the JV management emphasized the importance of employee training. Nevertheless, the Japanese partner had to make several adjustments to conditions in the United States. For example, weekly 'care meetings' between managers and operators (i.e. plant workers) were held. The Japanese management wanted operators to attend the meetings on their own time. However, they soon realized the reluctance of American workers to meet with management without being paid. As a result, operators were paid for time spent in the meetings.

The second case was classified as an American management style venture. The American parent made it clear in the initial discussions with its Japanese partner that it was not interested in forming a JV unless the American firm managed the JV. The American partner's vice president manufacturing argued, 'We have a quality reputation which we should be able to carry over to the JV.' Toward the end of the negotiating, the Japanese partner was still reluctant to concede management control. The American partner's attitude was, 'We are going to run this operation or we walk away from the JV.' Eventually, the Japanese partner agreed to its American partner's demands.

The Japanese partner's role was mainly concerned with marketing because the largest customers were the transplants. The American partner provided the plant manager, the process equipment, built the plant, and provided the accounting and finance systems for the JV. In return, the American partner received a management fee for running the plant. The plant was modelled on existing American parent plants and followed American parent procedures in areas such as human resources and computer systems. Nevertheless, the JV president conceded that the Japanese partner became more involved in the JV than initially planned. In his words, 'They wore us down and we finally agreed to let them put some sales people in the plant.'

The third case, a 50–50 ownership venture, was classified as a hybrid management style JV. Although the JV agreement stipulated that the American parent would provide the president and be responsible for day-to-day management control, when the venture was formed the partners agreed that it should be run like a Japanese company. There would be uniforms, open offices, consensus management, etc. According to a JV manager, 'The Japanese emphasis did not last long. For example, the open office concept did not work because there was not enough space and the lack of privacy was disconcerting.' The JV then went through a process of 'de-Japanization'. A new JV vice president was brought in from the American parent. The JV shifted from a Japanese management orientation to one that combined American and Japanese philosophies. Although manufacturing and marketing were largely based on Japanese processes, both the JV vice president and the plant manager emphasized, 'This is not a Japanese company; Japanese management would not work here.'

The management style classification yielded 12 Japanese, six American, and 22 hybrid JVs. Not surprisingly, the ventures classified as having a predominantly Japanese management style were closely associated with the Japanese automakers. Of the 11 JVs with single transplant customers, seven were considered Japanese management style ventures. Only two of the twelve Japanese style ventures dealt with US assemblers. On the other hand, all of the American management style ventures had domestic assemblers as customers (but only one dealt exclusively with domestic customers).

JV PERFORMANCE

JVs are formed when two or more partners, often with disparate skills and objectives, pool a portion of their resources to form a new entity. Consequently, JVs have a high potential for management conflict between the partners. As Killing pointed out, the primary problems in managing JVs stem from one cause: there is more than one parent (1982: 121). The owners of JVs are often visible and powerful; they can, and will, disagree on just about anything. Unlike licensing agreements or supplier relationships, contractual agreements between JV partners are often executed under conditions of high uncertainty. Therefore, it is unlikely that all future contingencies can be anticipated at the outset.

JV performance was measured from the perspective of the American parent. Based on the American parent's overall satisfaction with JV performance, the JVs were classified into three categories: failure, moderate success, and success. The JVs classified as failures were all cases of early or unplanned terminations that occurred because of serious problems in the working relationship between the partners. In the termination case not classified as a failure, termination occurred following the takeover of the American parent and a decision to sell the JV interest.

The JVs classified as moderate successes were still in existence but there was evidence of partner conflict. In particular, I looked for dissatisfaction with JV financial performance since this was a key determinant of satisfaction for the American partners. The JVs classified as successes were those with no outward signs of obvious partner conflicts. Plans for further partner commitments such as JV expansions or the formation of additional JVs provided evidence of a sound working relationship. While the successful JVs were not without conflict, they appeared to be functioning as going concerns and neither partner was considering termination. However, it is important to emphasize that longevity is not always a JV objective. Premature JV termination may be a mutual decision or it may be precipitated by the actions of one partner. For example, several cases were observed where one partner was clearly trying to learn from the other in order to erase dependency on that partner. The 'learning' partners and 'teaching' partners had very different longevity objectives.[7]

The performance classification resulted in 11 failures, 18 moderate successes, and 11 successes. One of the similarities across both successful and unsuccessful ventures was that financial performance was the key input in the American parent's evaluation of performance. As Anderson (1990) maintained, firms often evaluate their JVs using the same methods used to evaluate internal divisions. This situation existed for many American firms in this study. There was a tendency to treat the JVs as if they were in environments similar to the parent's domestic customer markets, with return on investment a key factor in evaluating the ventures.

A preoccupation with short-term financial issues was a common characteristic of the failed JVs. As one executive commented about anticipated JV performance, 'We thought we were well positioned to get transplant business. The JV would be a piece of cake; the transplants were like ducks on the pond.' Many American partner firms had trouble adjusting to the stringent demands of the transplants and were unprepared for the level of profit margins their JVs experienced as transplant suppliers. The American partners were generally unwilling to absorb losses to the same extent as their Japanese partners. Granted, the Japanese partners often had no choice but to remain associated with the JV organization because of long established supplier–manufacturer relationships in Japan.

Faced with lower than expected returns on investment and an information-poor environment, the American firms often reacted by questioning their original JV motives and the motives of their partners. Several managers' comments illustrate the profit concerns of the American partners:

> There can never be a meeting of minds on profit. The US partner wants to know when the JV will be profitable; the Japanese partner is more concerned with improving efficiency and satisfying their customer's needs.

> Americans will be committed to the JV as long as it is profitable. If it ceases to be profitable the commitment will disappear. The Japanese will remain committed as long as they believe there is room for improvement.

THE CREATION OF COMPETITORS

This study raises some interesting issues associated with JV termination. Two implications of termination are considered, while recognizing that the longevity of a JV should not be equated with JV success. One, JVs have significant downside risk in that should a venture be terminated, a competitor may be created. Two, an organization may view its JV as intentionally temporary, which means that the JV exists as a transitional organizational form.

When serious conflicts between the partners made termination of the JVs inevitable, the Japanese partners acquired their American partners' interest in all but one case. Of the twelve ventures that have or probably will be terminated, none involved dissolution of the JV business. In the one case where the American partner acquired full ownership of a terminated JV, the informant indicated that the Japanese partner had not abandoned the North American market and was planning a re-entry in another form. The other eleven JVs have, or probably will become wholly-owned subsidiaries of the Japanese partners.

For the terminated JVs that were transplant suppliers, the American partners conceded their share of the transplant market to their Japanese partners. In contrast, the Japanese firms remained committed to their North American investments and, rather than dissolving the JV organizations, became sole owners. By transferring their share of the JV to the Japanese partners, the American firms often created new competitors. Compounding the problem, the competitors had a state-of-the-art plant, a young workforce, and owners who were willing to endure substantial losses to gain a foothold in the North American automotive industry.

In several cases, the negative implications of creating a competitor were not recognized by the American parents until after the JV relationship became unmanageable. Other American parents recognized the risks of collaborating with a potential competitor and explicitly restricted the JV to transplant business or domestic business outside the American parent's primary product lines. Several American firms that originally restricted their ventures to transplant business later decided that, because of the JV's superior capabilities, the venture should be used as the basis for targeting new US automaker business. A JV executive explained the dilemma facing an American partner:

> The American partner is losing some of its domestic business. They are starting to consider how they might be able to use the JV to manufacture for the domestic OEMs while not completely turning over the business to the JV. The American partner does not want to create a monster that becomes a potential competitor in the event of a breakup.

JVs as transitional organizational forms

Managers in a few JVs indicated that they suspected the Japanese partners may have entered the JVs with the goal of acquiring full ownership several years later. This raises several questions. Were the Japanese partners in this study in a race to learn? And, were they intent on 'de-skilling' their American partners? In most cases the answer is probably no; the Japanese firms may have viewed the JVs as transitional but my observations suggest that most did not have an explicit goal of unsanctioned skill transfers. However, in a few cases the American partners did believe their Japanese partners had explicit objectives of learning quickly in order to make the JV obsolete, as comments from two managers illustrate:

The American partner did not understand what was needed to manage the JV. The Japanese partner knew exactly what was needed. I would not be surprised if the Japanese partner's original intention was to get their foot in the door by selecting a weak partner, get the JV started, and then take over the JV.

Our Japanese partner never did share their goals with us. They wanted a foothold in the United States which we could provide. They used us and then threw us away.

The American partners in this study may have underestimated the speed by which their Japanese partners would adapt to the North American environment. Similarly, General Motors may have underestimated the risks involved in forming a JV with Toyota (Badaracco 1991). The NUMMI JV was managed by Toyota, forcing Toyota managers to learn how to work with American workers and labour unions. Toyota then easily deployed its new knowledge in its wholly-owned plant in Georgetown, Kentucky.

To make the transition from JV to wholly-owned subsidiary, Toyota, and the Japanese firms in this study, had only to learn how to transfer an existing management process to North America. While many of the Japanese firms were initially uncertain about operating in North America, several years as part of a JV probably would allow the firms to acquire the necessary knowledge to compete autonomously. In contrast, the American firms trying to learn from their Japanese partners faced major changes in very fundamental operating philosophies. Thus, while Japanese JV partners were often seen as potential competitors by the American firms, none of the American partners studied was able to mount a genuine competitive threat to their Japanese partners.

CONCLUSION

The 1980s introduced North American automotive suppliers to a new set of competitive demands. Judging from the speed with which Japanese and other international firms have made inroads into the North American automotive industry, pressures for lower costs and higher quality will continue to escalate. One aspect of the changing industry structure is the large number of Japanese–North American JVs at the supplier level. Many North American firms, recognizing the implications of a growing Japanese automaker presence, have seen a JV with a Japanese firm as the only means of gaining access to this growing market segment. Thus, a JV strategy offers the advantages of timeliness and efficiency in transplant market access for American firms.

Unfortunately, the JVs have often performed far below expectations. From an American partner perspective, the characteristic that was most evident across the sample of JVs was unsatisfactory JV performance. Although it is overly simplistic to describe Japanese management as long-term oriented and American management as short-term oriented, the Japanese partner firms in this study appeared to focus on customer satisfaction and product quality rather than profit-based performance.[8] Consistent with many articles written over the past few years (e.g. Doyle *et al.* 1992; Keys *et al.* 1994), the Japanese firms seemed less constrained by issues of share price and impatient boards of directors than their American counterparts. From the American partner perspective, problems with financial performance contributed significantly to JV instability.

When the JVs were strongly involved with Japanese transplants as customers, performance problems were often more pronounced. This is supported by the finding that satisfaction with JV performance was stronger when the primary JV motive was not transplant customer access. The JVs that were more 'Japanized' also seemed to experience greater performance difficulties, probably because the Japanese emphasis was less on financial performance and more on customer satisfaction.

Clearly, if American firms are to exploit successfully JV strategies with Japanese partners, they must become more tolerant of partner expectations, particularly those involving financial performance. A defensive, short-term perspective may be one that is inevitably subject to failure. The successful JVs in this study were generally those in which the American partner adopted a long-term strategic perspective. This position is explained by a JV manager:

> The [JV] relationship must be formed with the objective of creating a stronger company than could have been created by going it alone. If the JV is created just to protect a weakening domestic market the JV will probably fail. The partners have to have similar goals and those goals should be 'to be the best'.

Chapter 3

The role of Japanese networks

In the previous chapter, reference was made to the Japanese partners' membership in supplier groups. A significant difference between Japanese and American corporate environments is the extensive network of intercorporate agreements between firms in Japan. Within this network of alliances or *keiretsu*, trust and loyalty play key roles in creating an environment of reciprocal expectations (Kester 1991). While questions remain about the degree to which the *keiretsu* system is efficient or merely exclusionist, network affiliations exert a powerful influence on the behaviours and strategies of Japanese firms.

Japanese networks developed as a response to institutional and competitive pressures that traditionally have been thought of as uniquely Japanese. However, the network system has been successfully transferred outside Japan. In particular, the movement of the Japanese automotive firms and their suppliers to the United States has, according to Florida and Kenney (1991: 394), 'shown little sign of conforming to the US model of organization'. Instead, the Japanese automakers with North American 'transplant' manufacturing operations have replicated the Japanese network model of supplier tiers and interfirm relationships. By replicating what had been considered a uniquely Japanese form of organizing, the Japanese transplants have set new standards for North American automobile manufacturing.

With Japanese networks taking root in the American business environment, what does this mean for American firms competing and cooperating with Japanese firms? This chapter examines this question by looking at the structure and underlying rationale of Japanese networks and the implications for American firms associated with the networks. In the chapter's first section, an overview of Japanese corporate networks is provided, emphasizing corporate relationships in the automotive industry. The second section analyses the transfer of

Japanese networks to North America. The analysis focuses on two main areas: one, the Japanese network as a barrier to entry for 'outsider' firms and two, the economic efficiency of the network system. The third section considers the implications for outsider firms gaining temporary, and perhaps even permanent access to the network through the formation of JVs with Japanese firms. This section describes problems US managers have encountered when confronted with the perceived ambiguity and uncertainty of Japanese networks. Several factors contributing to the ability of American JV firms to control their network affiliations are identified.

THE JAPANESE AUTOMOTIVE NETWORKS

In examining Japanese networks,[1] three underlying patterns can be identified. This network categorization scheme, developed by Gerlach (1992a), includes:

1 inter-corporate alliances based on historical relationships;
2 bank-centred groups;
3 interdependence among industrial firms, such as the management of vertical relationships.

While there are overlapping attributes among the three types of inter-corporate relationships, each pattern should be viewed as an important organizing form in the Japanese economy. The primary focus of this chapter is on the third pattern: industrial interdependencies and, in particular, manufacturer–supplier relationships in which a large manufacturer coordinates the vertical activities of a core group of suppliers. This type of network, also called an enterprise group, is the focal point for Japanese competition. The various enterprise groups compete fiercely with one another and expect complete loyalty from their member firms. The large firms have a paternalistic relationship with the lower-level organizations, often financing their activities and providing management personnel, training, and education.

The Japanese automobile industry illustrates how a network of largely industrial interdependencies can evolve into an institutionalized arrangement. There are eleven vehicle manufacturers in Japan, each controlling a network of sub-suppliers through a system of 'vertical contractual dependence' (Turnbull 1989). The sub-suppliers are organized into tiers. The first-tier suppliers coordinate the operations of many smaller second-tier suppliers; the second-tier suppliers in turn work with their sub-suppliers. The result is a pyramid-like structure with the automakers sitting on top. The automakers deal mainly with first-tier suppliers; these suppliers are usually 'sole suppliers' in product development and design work. For example, Toyota has about 170 first-tier suppliers, 5,500 second-tier suppliers, and more than 40,000 third-tier suppliers (Fruin 1992). The responsibility for quality is pushed down through the tiers; the first tier is responsible for the second tier, the second tier for the third tier, and so on. In this way, the span of control remains manageable at the different levels.

The Japanese automakers are essentially assemblers of automobiles, relying on their suppliers for complex sub-assemblies. About 80 per cent of a Japanese automobile's cost comes from outside suppliers, in contrast to only 50 to 60 per cent in France, Germany, and the United States (Odaka et al. 1988).

For their transplant operations, the Japanese automakers had a choice between importing parts from Japan or encouraging their suppliers to move to the United States. To the extent possible, the automakers chose the latter because of high importing costs and because of US political pressures against importing. What is interesting is that manufacturing the parts in-house was not an option because the Japanese automakers do not have the expertise to carry out extensive in-house parts and components manufacturing.[2]

While it is true that the Japanese automakers rely much less on in-house suppliers than do their North American counterparts, Japanese manufacturer–supplier relationships often assume characteristics similar to the in-house parts divisions of the North American automakers. These relationships resemble a form of quasi-integration by the assemblers. Supplier group members are given preferential treatment for new business and participate actively in the design and engineering process. The automotive assembler has access to internal supplier information and may help finance supplier capital investment. These types of manufacturer–supplier interactions are the foundation for the reciprocal expectations that exist in the Japanese corporate networks.

Within the manufacturer–supplier networks there is a complex mix of information-sharing, cooperation, and competition. Information-sharing among suppliers is especially important. The Japanese automakers encourage their first-tier suppliers to coordinate their activities and, within limits, share information about product design and costs. For example, Toyota's first-tier suppliers are organized into a group known as *Kyoho-kai* – roughly translated as a club for co-prospering with Toyota (Dodwell 1990: 36). While there is some sharing of suppliers between the major manufacturers, Nissan's suppliers depend on Nissan for over 90 per cent of their business and the dependency of Toyota suppliers is about 65 per cent (Turnbull *et al.* 1992). In some cases, the automakers have an ownership stake in their suppliers and may provide them with financial assistance. These financial ties reinforce intragroup trading patterns (Fruin 1992). However, Fruin also argued that financial ties are not the answer to why Japanese firms work together. In the case of Toyota, its investment in suppliers is significant in only a few cases and Toyota rarely, if ever, invests in second- or third-tier companies.

Why have the Japanese firms tended to use subcontracting and long-term relationships much more extensively than non-Japanese companies? An argument could be made that it allows the primary manufacturers to withdraw supply contracts when demands for final products weaken. The suppliers then become a buffer for cyclical down-turns in the automotive industry. In North America, automotive suppliers have long complained that the Big Three automakers practise this type of exploitation on weaker supplier firms. However, in Japan there is often a clear demarcation of tasks between the primary manu-facturer and its sub-suppliers (Aoki 1990). As the suppliers assume a greater role in product design and development, the primary manu-facturer may be unable to sever a relationship because a disruption could be very costly for the manufacturer. Over time, primary manufacturers and suppliers become very interdependent, with mutual trust being the glue which cements the relationships.

THE NETWORKS AND JV FORMATION

The Japanese networks played a key role in the decisions of the Japanese JV firms to invest in North America. To a much greater extent than in North America, Japanese suppliers are expected to do what is necessary to meet the needs of their primary customers. If the transplants build a plant in North America, suppliers must follow or risk upsetting a long-standing customer relationship in Japan. Consequently, much of the investment by Japanese automotive suppliers in North America has not followed the western notion of capital investment. It is unlikely that the Japanese suppliers treated the potential return on investment from a North American facility as the primary decision-making criterion. Instead, Japanese automakers expected their suppliers to follow them to North America and the suppliers realized they had little choice.[3]

It is important to recognize, however, that Japanese manufacturers do not guarantee business to their long-term suppliers. Japanese firms strive to maintain a trade-off between long-term relationships and competition between suppliers (Kester 1991). Supplier rivalry is maintained by the careful collection and comparison of supplier information (Smitka 1991). As long as suppliers can continue to match their competitor's delivery and quality standards and price, repeat business is assured. If a supplier's standards decrease, business may be lost. However, suppliers are expected to inform their automaker customers of anticipated problems and must be willing to tolerate what would appear to American firms as meddling by the customer in its supplier's business. In the automotive industry, contracts are usually given to suppliers for the life of a part. When there is a model change, existing suppliers will have an inside track for new model parts but no guarantee (Smitka 1991).

Given the lack of guaranteed business, Japanese suppliers' investments in North America have not been without risk. Several JVs studied were formed with the expectation of transplant contracts that did not materialize. While the Japanese partners expected transplant market access because of their existing relationships in Japan, it was not guaranteed. Nevertheless, a key to the transplants' success in North America has been the willingness of Japanese suppliers to invest in North America to support new assembly operations. Many of these investments were made without any formal commitments from the Japanese automakers.[4]

Another important point regarding Japanese manufacturer–supplier relationships is that Japanese suppliers in North America are often free to compete for business outside their primary customer segment. While several JVs in the study were explicitly tied to a single transplant and effectively prevented from pursuing new customers, most ventures were actively developing new business. For many Japanese firms in North America, an explicit goal is to become a supplier to the US automakers. A link with an American firm is often perceived as a key factor in achieving that goal because if the JV, through its American partner's connections, can become a US automaker supplier, the Japanese firm will have the opportunity to learn about the US automotive market.

THE NETWORK: A BARRIER TO ENTRY?

North American firms wishing to become transplant suppliers have, until fairly recently, faced formidable barriers stemming from a lack of experience with Japanese manufacturing processes. When the transplants first arrived in North America in the early 1980s, many supplier firms were unfamiliar with the rigours of just-in-time systems, demands for flexible production, and assembler expectations regarding supplier involvement in product development. However, as US automakers move closer to the Japanese production model, these factors have become less important as barriers for North American suppliers seeking access to the transplant market.

A key question associated with the large-scale movement of Japanese manufacturers to North America is the extent to which Japanese suppliers receive preferential treatment because of manufacturer–supplier relationships that exist in Japan. Specifically, is the Japanese network a barrier to entry for outsiders? Within the automotive industry, the existence of Japanese automotive supplier groups within a larger network structure has been identified as the fundamental reason American firms have been largely unsuccessful in capturing a larger share of the transplant business. For example, Harold Poling, CEO Ford Motor Company, was quoted, 'it's unfortunate that the Japanese don't attempt to utilize the domestic suppliers, but want to use Japanese, or Japanese transplant suppliers' (Kahalas and Suchon 1992: 73).

For the American firms in this study, the primary JV motive in 29 of 40 cases was access to the transplant market. The predominant opinion of the American managers was that American firm access to the transplant market would not have been possible without a Japanese connection. In other words, American firms saw their outsider status as a barrier to entering the transplant market. There was a strong belief that the Japanese transplants wanted to deal with Japanese suppliers and were willing to sacrifice the locational experience of American suppliers and even the potentially lower costs of American suppliers. Given this belief, a Japanese JV partner was viewed as the most effective and timely means of acquiring the connection that would enable the American firms to become transplant suppliers.

If the Japanese network is an entry barrier, is it consistent with the barrier concept used by business strategy scholars? Barriers to entry are often discussed as the outcome of firm strategic decisions that create imperfectly imitable resources (McGee and Thomas 1986). Porter (1980) identified six major sources of entry barriers: economies of scale, product differentiation, capital requirements, switching costs, access to distribution channels, and cost disadvantages independent of scale. These barriers have several properties in common. Of particular interest is the notion that the firm's strategic decisions can have a major impact on the strength and durability of entry barriers (Barney 1991; Porter 1980). For an entry barrier to exist, firms protected by barriers must be implementing different strategies than firms seeking to enter the protected areas of competition (Barney 1991). If exclusion from an industry or group is not by choice, the firms outside the barrier must be unable to implement the same strategies as firms within an industry or group. Therefore, the outsider firms must not have the same resources as firms within the industry or group.

Following this perspective, the Japanese firms in the network must possess strategically relevant resources that American suppliers (the outsiders) do not have. There is evidence that US suppliers can work effectively with Japanese automakers if given the opportunity, suggesting that a lack of skills is not the hurdle facing US suppliers trying to gain access to the transplant market (Cusumano and Takeishi 1991). If specific skills are not the barrier to entry, the group itself must be the barrier, with group membership providing the protection from outside competitors. The 'resource' controlled by the protected members is membership. Overcoming the barrier means gaining membership in the supplier network, dislodging an existing member, and establishing a favourable reputation with automaker customers. Positive reputations between customers and suppliers have been cited as sources of competitive advantage and, therefore, are potentially imperfectly imitable (Porter 1980). However, reputation results after entry into a market and is the result of the implementation of successful strategic decisions that, in Porter's view, increase the value added to the customer. Indeed, Porter's (1985) advice concerning supplier selection is primarily concerned with selecting suppliers that are the most efficient or offer the lowest cost.

Clearly, a firm in a Japanese network must have a good reputation to remain in the network. However, the Japanese network goes beyond reputation because, unlike North American companies, Japanese automakers rarely change suppliers. For example, Toyota's supplier base has remained almost unchanged since the 1950s. The president of Nissan's US operations explained:

> Nissan's mix of US suppliers and Japanese suppliers is not likely to change much. Given our philosophy, once you become our supplier you're our supplier forever on that part, unless you mess up so bad we can't fix you.

> (Miller and Winter 1991: 29)

Certainty and durability are two factors that make the Japanese network significantly different from the Western notion of positive reputation as a basis for competitive advantage. While there is a complex set of overlapping boundaries within the networks, relative to the loose American corporate networks, the Japanese networks are

coherent, well-ordered, and long-term arrangements (Gerlach 1992b). Penetrating the network is, as many American firms have discovered, very difficult. Membership in the network confers on the network members a unique firm resource that, at least in Japan, can be sustainable for decades. However, the question remains as to the efficiency of the network. If the network is efficient in generating low cost for the firms at the top of the pyramid, the status of the network as an entry barrier may include an additional complicating factor for prospective entrants. This issue is considered in the next section.

THE EFFICIENCY OF THE NETWORK

For the primary manufacturers (those at the top of the pyramid), there seems little doubt that the system is efficient in terms of administrative cost. In the automotive industry, if the automakers and top-tier suppliers change suppliers, additional costs are incurred because new 'uninformed' members have to be introduced to the norms of the network. However, in the automakers' product sourcing equation, administrative cost is probably less critical than the direct costs associated with manufacturing, quality, and delivery.

The reluctance of the Japanese transplants to expand rapidly their local content has been a major political issue in Japanese–United States trade negotiations. The transplants have argued that North American suppliers are unable to meet their product quality, design, engineering, and delivery demands. Not surprisingly, the North American suppliers tend to reject this argument, contending that their network outsider status has kept them from becoming transplant suppliers.

The JV managers interviewed tended to support the view that North American firms were unable to meet transplant demands. As evidence, these managers argued that the products manufactured in the JVs were far superior to those manufactured by the American parents. A comment from a manager illustrates this point:

> The product manufactured in the JV is superior to anything made in other American partner plants. An American plant probably would consider it a perfect month if they were on time for all their shipments and had only five rejects. Our transplant customer will look at the five rejects and say, 'there are five problems so you have a quality problem'.

Despite the quality differences that existed between American parents and their JVs, it is important to note that JV manufacturing superiority does not necessarily mean North American parent firms lack the skills to supply transplants. As Cusumano and Takeishi (1991) found, the transplant customers demand more in terms of quality than US automakers. On average, US firms supplying both US and transplant automakers were providing their transplant customers with higher quality than their US customers (Cusumano and Takeishi 1991).

Cusumano and Takeishi's study supports the arguments made by American industry representatives that, given the chance, American suppliers could meet the demands of the transplants. While definitive conclusions about the network's economic efficiency await further research, Cusumano's and Takeishi's findings and the evidence from this study raise questions about the extent to which the Japanese network form of manufacturer–supplier management contributes to manufacturing performance. Researchers have documented the importance of the network from an administrative perspective and, in particular, how the Japanese environment is the basis for stable, long-term relationships. For example, Smitka (1991) provided a detailed analysis of the process of socializing new network members in Japan.

However, there is a need for further research on the efficiency of the Japanese network in a non-Japanese context. The more competitive and open business environment in North America may negate some of the network's manufacturing advantages that exist in Japan. An opinion expressed by several JV managers in the current study was that the transplant customers were incurring higher costs than necessary to keep their business in the network. The following comment from an American manager supports this position:

> The JV product is higher quality but it also has a higher cost. The quality is higher because 1) the design is different (there are more parts) and 2) the manufacturing process is superior. The higher cost is attributable to a combination of lower volume and a better design . . . . Although the JV designs and quality are superior to the parent's product, the JV will never be competitive with the traditional sources [large American producers] because of its higher cost base.

Another American manager was convinced that had he been allowed to develop the JV's supplier base, several million dollars a year could have been saved. Instead, the Japanese partner insisted on using network members wherever possible and, in the American manager's opinion, was overpaying for its purchases. The Japanese partner's argument was that selecting new and untried suppliers was a high-risk strategy.

Trust as economic pragmatism

Earlier, mutual trust and cooperation were identified as central to the stability of Japanese networks. An argument often made is that trust and cooperation between Japanese companies are cultural artifacts of Japanese society (e.g. see Yoshida, 1992). However, an alternate viewpoint gaining increasing acceptance is that trust and interfirm ties in Japan are motivated by economic factors and therefore should be viewed not as cultural but as a form of economic pragmatism (Kester 1991; Smitka 1991). This section explores the notion of trust as economic pragmatism and offers an assessment of the Japanese and American perspectives of trust.

The JV study provides an insight into the role of trust in the Japanese network. The different attitudes toward trust for the American and Japanese JV partners influenced the JV management process. Dependence is a key aspect of Japanese corporate relationships and contributes to the strength of supplier–manufacturer agreements. Once a relationship built on trust and mutual dependence is developed, both sides will generally attempt to make the relationship work. When dependence diminishes on either side, attitudes about the importance of a long-term relationship will probably change. Not surprisingly then, for the Japanese partner firms, trust appeared synonymous with long-term relationships and was closely related with the notion of dependence.

In contrast, the American firms viewed trust as important because it allowed the partners to work together and rely on one another to operate within the spirit of the agreement. However, the presence of trust was generally not linked to the establishment of a long-term relationship. An American partner with complete trust in its Japanese partner might still wish to sell its share of the JV for financial reasons. To the American firm this would be good business; to the Japanese it would be a breach of trust because it failed to acknowledge mutual dependence and the importance of long-term relationships. Several American managers suggested that the Japanese focused too much on trust rather than good business sense (good business sense was defined, of course, from an American perspective). However, these managers failed to recognize that the Japanese focus on trust, although different from the American perspective, was grounded in economic pragmatism. Trust is viewed as essential for long-term relationships and long-term relationships are seen as good business.

The different trust perspectives were evident in several cases where the American partner wanted to terminate the JV. The Japanese firms were shocked and offended when they realized their American partners wanted to break the relationship. In a specific case, the American partner wished to reduce its equity from 60 per cent to 20 per cent, primarily for financial reasons. A JV executive described the response of the Japanese partner:

> Initially, the American partner was not trying to end the JV. They talked about 20 per cent ownership [with the Japanese partner holding the other 80 per cent]. However, the Japanese partner was shocked that its American partner was considering reducing its commitment to the venture. Once the Japanese partner knew that its American partner was unhappy with the existing relationship, they felt that changing the ownership structure would not help a relationship that was obviously in trouble. The Japanese partner made the drive to take over the JV completely. Their attitude was, 'Why bother to stay in the JV when there is no longer any trust between the partners?' They took it as an affront that the American partner would want to break the relationship.

In the previous example, the Japanese partner adopted the perspective that the relationship was built on trust and, despite some problems, the two partners had agreed to work together and should attempt to solve their problems before changing the relationship structure. As the JV executive commented, 'The Japanese partner would never have brought up the problems and would have stayed in the JV for 50 years.' However, once the American partner openly indicated dissatisfaction with the JV, the Japanese partner concluded that there was no longer mutual trust between the partners. In contrast, the issue of trust appeared not to be a major factor in the American partner's decision. Dissatisfaction with venture performance was the primary factor in the decision.

AMERICAN FIRMS AND NETWORK MEMBERSHIP STATUS

Network theory suggests that a firm entering a network must position itself among the established members. Likewise, existing members may have to reposition themselves to accommodate the new member (Thorelli 1986). When an American firm forms a JV with a Japanese firm, it becomes a part of its partner's complex network of relationships, albeit a somewhat tentative member. This section examines some of the issues facing American firms that gained involuntary membership status in Japanese networks.

Managers in a *keiretsu* firm are influenced by a complex interaction of control and monitoring by customers, other suppliers, and banks, all of whom may have long-term contractual relationships with the firm besides being major creditors and shareholders (Prowse 1992). The unfamiliarity of most American managers with the norms of network membership often created a sense of frustration and uncertainty. A JV executive described the relationship between the Japanese partner and the JV:

> Gradually, we realized that our partner had a hidden agenda that we would never be able to understand. They [the Japanese partner] saw the JV as advertising; they were willing to lose money to maintain their Japanese relationship. That relationship was beyond anything we could get a handle on.

Another manager in an American firm involved in a venture with a large trading company stated:

> We are not used to doing business with a trading company. We are not sure who is in charge in the trading company because we do not understand the network. The Japanese partner has many different divisions; it is incredibly complex.

Hamada's (1991) detailed study of a US–Japanese JV based in Japan also revealed that the American managers, at the time the venture was formed, had a very limited understanding of the workings of Japanese networks. These managers were surprised to learn the extent to which the JV's Japanese managers considered themselves part of the *keiretsu* group. Managerial codes of behaviour were based on group norms and managers considered themselves employees of the group as opposed to JV employees. While the American managers were charged with profit-making responsibilities in the ventures, the Japanese managers had very different objectives. One of these objectives was to maintain good relationships with other group members and, in particular, the large firm at the top of the group.

In the current study, the product pricing area was particularly difficult for American managers to deal with. A dissatisfaction with the pricing structure of the JV products was a major source of conflict between the JV partners, particularly when the JV dealt only with transplants. When the JV customers were transplants and the products sold by the JVs were duplicates of products made in Japan (most of the cases in the study), American managers often indicated that they had limited knowledge about how initial prices were determined for the JV products. Usually, the price was based on an agreement between the Japanese partner and the transplant using the price in Japan as the target price.[5] This price, at least initially, was not necessarily related to the cost of manufacturing the part in North America and the American partners usually found themselves excluded from discussions of price and profit margins.

Because the American partners' only network link with the Japanese automakers was through the JV, there were few opportunities to benefit through contractual adjustments that were not price-related. Unlike the Japanese partners with their long-standing relationships to consider, the American partners were new to the network and quasi-members at best. Thus, armed with little or no knowledge about how the initial product prices were determined and a profit situation often deemed unsatisfactory, a typical American partner reaction was 'we need to renegotiate the price with the transplants'.

Not surprisingly, the Japanese partners had a very different perspective. Because the Japanese partners' network connections went beyond formal contracts for specific parts, the last thing the Japanese firms needed or wanted to do was force a confrontation over price. Price adjustments are not the way Japanese companies usually solve conflicts. Clear standards for pricing, quality, delivery, and ordering exist in Japan, creating a type of orderly competition largely unfamiliar to the west (Smitka 1991). Forcing a confrontation about a pricing issue may be relatively common in North America but in Japan it rarely happens between manufacturers and long-term suppliers. Haggling about prices occurs, but usually not with a confrontational tone. To be confrontational in Japan is to be seen as insincere, which disrupts the 'ordered harmony' (Sullivan 1992). As a manager noted:

> In Japan, our Japanese partner does not compete head-to-head. Head-to-head competition takes place between 'mother' [the automaker] and the other Japanese OEMs [automakers]. Mother tells the sibling to be good and we will take care of you. Getting involved in tough price competition in the United States was something new for our partner and made it hard for them to take the pricing issue seriously. In Japan the price is set gentlemanly.

Nevertheless, price confrontations were forced in several cases because the American partners decided the prices negotiated in Japan were unrealistic in an American environment. Without a price increase, they argued, the JV could not survive. In one situation, after much discussion the Japanese partner agreed that the pricing issue had to be raised with the transplant. However, as the JV president explained, the Japanese partner preferred to remain in the background.

I was willing to force a confrontation because in my opinion, the transplant would not be able to find another supplier with better prices, even with the increase. However, the Japanese partner wants American parent executives to take the lead with the pricing issue so they can blame the American parent as the bad guys in the dispute. The Japanese partner would never directly threaten its primary transplant customer.

Network demands and JV success

The implication that emerges from the previous discussion is that if American firms want to succeed in their relationships with Japanese firms, they should takes steps to control and understand network affiliations. From the JV study, two factors were identified that contributed to the American firms' ability to control their network affiliations. The first factor is very straightforward: experience and knowledge of the Japanese environment. In this study there were 24 ventures where the partners had been involved in a prior relationship. In most cases, prior relationships involved technology sharing and licensing agreements, many beginning in the 1960s with the American firm transferring technology to Japan. Over the years, the agreements often evolved into two-way arrangements. In several cases, technology sharing agreements resulted in the American and Japanese firms agreeing not to compete with each other in their home markets. These non-competition agreements provided the impetus for the formation of several JVs. In a few JVs, prior partner relationships involved personal relationships between senior managers rather than explicit business arrangements.

While a prior relationship cannot guarantee that a firm develops an understanding of its partner's network ties, at a minimum it provides a foundation for insight into the Japanese business environment. The second important factor that allowed American firms to control and manage their entry into the network was the nature of partner contributions to the venture and, in particular, the relationship between contributions and bargaining power. A partner firm that has the option to contribute or withhold an important resource or input for the venture can use that option as leverage in bargaining with its partner. In turn, the partner holding the bargaining power has access to more available partners than does the partner with limited bargaining power (Yan and Gray 1994).

In many of the ventures studied, American partner contributions were limited to infrastructure and functional management support. The critical strategic contributions of customer access, manufacturing technology, and general management were made by the Japanese partner. When the American partner was able to make strategic contributions, its bargaining power with its partner increased and, accordingly, its bargaining power in the network also increased. While the nature of the ventures generally precluded the American partners from contributing customer access, several firms insisted on contributing the general management role. By influencing the venture's strategic direction through general management, American firms were less likely to be excluded from decisions driven by network affiliations and were more likely to develop some insider perspectives. Of course, general management responsibility can have its downside. A manager described a problem associated with general management control:

> We get blamed for being American. We don't have a Japanese manager on the floor so any little hiccup in terms of quality is blamed on us. We are always hearing [from our Japanese customers] 'that never happens in Japan'.

CONCLUSION

As non-Japanese firms continue to invest in Japan and establish business relationships with Japanese firms outside of Japan, understanding the structure and underlying rationale of Japanese networks will become critical. Japanese industrial interdependencies extend far beyond American notions of customer–supplier relationships. Networks in Japan are the dominant factor in determining how firms transact with other organizations and the building and maintenance of networks is of far greater importance than is generally the case in the West.

The extent to which Japanese networks have evolved as the result of economic and/or cultural factors is an interesting and unresolved question. If the assumption is made that the networks have their roots in economic motives, a further question is whether the economic motives hold true when the network is transferred outside Japan. In the case of the automotive industry, the willingness of suppliers to follow their automaker customers to North America has been a key factor in the transplants' success. Thus, from the transplant automakers' perspectives, the networks have supported an efficient transfer of skills to their North American operations. In fact, the speed of the transfer probably caught the US automakers off guard.

The network as a cultural artifact also has some credence, particularly given the manner in which the network acts as an entry barrier for outsider firms. In the JV study, transplant access was the primary JV motive for American partners. Access to the transplant market was perceived as closed to non-Japanese (or non-network) firms, suggesting that cultural factors may be involved.

By forming JVs with Japanese firms, American firms can become involved in the networks of their partners. However, the set of mutual expectations that governs the relationship between the Japanese partners and their network affiliates will not extend to the tentative network status of the American firms. Consequently, the uncertainty and ambiguity associated with the American partners' network membership can contribute to conflict between the partners, particularly in areas such as product pricing and quality control. In cases where firms had previous experience with Japanese firms or could increase their bargaining power in the JVs, the uncertainty associated with the networks was mitigated to some degree.

Although the structure of Japanese networks may look like illegal cartels and unfair competition to the non-Japanese observer (e.g. see Kearns 1992), networks and *keiretsu* are a way of life in Japan.[6] Cutts (1992), citing a Japanese Fair Trade Commission report, reported that almost 90 per cent of all Japanese domestic business transactions are among parties involved in a long-standing relationship of some sort. As well, Japanese business transactions outside Japan are also likely to involve network relationships. Although the North American branches of the automotive networks have existed for only a decade or so, and as such their durability, stability, and efficiency have yet to be determined, there is evidence that the transfer of the networks outside Japan has been successfully accomplished. As similar scenarios unfold in other industries and American firms increase their presence in Japan, managers should be aware of and appreciate the important role of Japanese networks.

Chapter 4

The control and performance of international JVs

This chapter was written with additional data provided by Shigefumi Makino

---

A prominent theme in the literature on international JVs is the relationship between JV control and performance. However, prior research in this area has yielded inconclusive results. In addition, in much of the IJV literature, the national culture of JV partners and its impact on the collaborative process has not been addressed. A failure to consider the role of national culture in the collaborative process may impede efforts to develop a deeper understanding of core JV concepts, including performance and control. In this chapter, JV control and performance are examined using both the survey data and an additional sample of Japanese JVs.

THEORETICAL BACKGROUND

By definition, JVs create the potential for management conflict. JVs are formed when two or more partners, often with disparate skills and objectives, pool a portion of their resources to form a new entity. As Killing (1982: 121) pointed out, the primary problems in managing JVs stem from one cause: there is more than one parent. The owners of JVs are often visible and powerful; they can and will disagree on just about anything. Given the potential for partner conflict, control issues are usually an important consideration for JV partners. However, in comparison with wholly-owned subsidiaries, exercising effective control over JVs is often difficult for the parent firms, especially if they are unable to rely solely on their ownership position (Geringer and Hebert 1989).

Various approaches have been employed in an effort to develop an understanding of JV control and, in particular, its relationship with JV performance. Geringer and Hebert (1989) made a significant contribution in analysing the approaches and identifying three dimensions of control:

1 the mechanisms used by the parents to exercise control;
2 the extent of control achieved by the parents;
3 the scope of activities over which parents exercise control.

While Geringer and Hebert argued that the dimensions are complementary and interdependent, there is a paucity of empirical work to support their arguments. Thus, the objective of this chapter is to examine the different dimensions and their relationship with JV performance.

The control–performance relationship

A variety of mechanisms is available to parents for exercising effective control. Of these, JV ownership has most widely been investigated as the basis for establishing parent control. While ownership and control do not correspond perfectly (Hennart 1991), majority ownership provides the basis for a high degree of management control.

Blodgett (1992), using ownership to measure control, and stability to measure performance, found that 50–50 shared management arrangements had a greater chance for long life than majority-owned ventures.[1] Also using financial ownership as the indicator of decision-making control, Bleeke and Ernst (1991) concluded that alliances with an even split of ownership were more likely to succeed than those in which one partner held a majority interest. Blodgett and Bleeke and Ernst all offered commitment as the supporting rationale for their findings. When partners have equal ownership, there will be pressure on both sides to make accommodations to the JV to protect their investments and, therefore, both partners will be committed to making the venture successful. In a majority-owned venture, one partner may have the ability to configure the venture in a manner that is undesirable to the other partner(s).

Conceptualizing control in terms of the locus of decision-making and the extent of control exercised by partner firms provides the basis for an alternative view of performance and control. Killing (1982) identified three categories of JVs based on the extent of shared decision-making: dominant parent, shared management, and independent ventures. The primary determinant of the JV type was the degree of parent involvement in the decision-making of the JVs and the extent to which both parents had active roles.

In some cases, a partner may play a limited role because of a lack of relevant managerial skills or knowledge to contribute to the venture. In those circumstances, a dominant parent JV may be formed in which all the JV's operating and strategic decisions are made by dominant parent executives. In a shared venture, both parents play a meaningful managerial role. In an independent venture, the JV operates autonomously from both parents.

In making the link between control and performance, Killing (1982) found that dominant partner JVs were more likely to be successful than shared partner ventures. Killing argued that when a single parent controlled the venture's activities, the risks associated with coordination and potential conflicts were reduced. Therefore, dominant partner JVs will be easier to manage and consequently more successful. While there is conflicting evidence about this relationship (see the study by Beamish and Banks (1987) of developing country JVs), Killing's argument is persuasive, especially when interpreted within a transaction cost framework. Coordination between partners entails significant costs that make many alliances transitional rather than stable arrangements (Porter 1990). Reducing the risks associated with coordination can minimize transaction costs and stabilize the JV. Following this logic, JVs in which a dominant partner has decision-making control should perform better than ventures where control is shared.

Schaan (1983) argued that rather than considering the overall extent of control, it may be more meaningful to measure parent control over specific areas and activities.[2] A challenge from an empirical perspective is determining what activities should be examined, particularly if there is wide variation in the design and goals of the sample JVs. A promising avenue is to view control over organizational activities from the perspective of bargaining power, which in turn is a function of relative dependency on the partner(s).

The role of bargaining power and dependence was developed by Emerson (1962) and generalized to the organizational level in the resource-dependence model by Pfeffer and Salancik (1978). Possession of key resources by one entity may make other organizations dependent on that entity. In a cooperative relationship, dependence can be a source of power for the firm controlling the key resources because, to some degree, each firm can increase, or withhold, resources which are attractive to its partner (Bacharach and Lawler 1980). A firm that has the option to contribute or withhold an important resource or input can use that option as leverage in bargaining with its partner. As well, the partner holding the bargaining power has access to more available partners than does the partner with limited bargaining power (Yan and Gray 1994).

When one firm controls an 'irreplaceable' JV resource or input, a dependency situation is created. For the firm that does not control the input, a lack of bargaining power in this area is potentially a key factor in the evaluation of JV performance. The rationale is that if a firm lacks bargaining power over a strategic JV area, the firm may perceive that it cannot influence the JV's output and performance. Firms are unlikely to be satisfied with JV performance if the performance outcome is a function of the partner's responsibility to manage and control a key JV task. Thus, the control–performance relationship may be contingent on control over JV areas or activities.

Clearly, as Geringer and Hebert concluded: the relationship between dominant control and IJV performance appears to be far more complex and less direct than scholars originally perceived (1989: 245). A further complicating factor is the nature of JV performance. Because JVs are formed for a variety of purposes (Contractor and Lorange 1988; Hennart 1988) and often in highly uncertain settings, performance evaluation becomes a very difficult task (Anderson 1990). One perspective argues that JV performance should be evaluated as a mutual outcome and take into account the perspectives of the multiple partners (Beamish 1988). A different perspective suggests that performance should be viewed in terms of value creation. Because each partner will have different cooperative objectives and abilities to appropriate JV benefits, researchers should focus on the individual monetary and competitive gains of each partner (Hamel 1991). A further perspective is that JVs should be evaluated as stand-alone entities seeking to maximize their own performance, not the partners' (Anderson 1990). Finally, some researchers have used JV stability as an indicator of performance (Gomes-Casseres 1987; Kogut 1989).

AN EXAMINATION OF THE CONTROL–PERFORMANCE RELATIONSHIP

To examine the control–performance relationship, two analyses are presented. The first examines the relationship between ownership and performance and uses data from a separate sample of Japanese JVs. The second analysis uses the primary survey data.

Analysis One

The data for the first analysis came from a survey of Japanese JVs in the United States at the end of 1991. This data was collected by Toyo Keizai Shinposha, a Tokyo-based economics magazine publisher and one of the two largest collectors of Japanese corporate data in Japan. The survey is based on questionnaires sent to all the Japanese companies, both those listed on the Japanese stock market and unlisted firms, that have foreign direct investment (FDI).[3] The database covers about 14,000 cases (in 1992) out of 67,800 worldwide FDI cases recognized by the Japan Ministry of Finance in 1992.

From the sample of JVs in the Toyo Keizai database, JVs in the United States with one Japanese partner and one local partner were selected. The analysis was restricted to two partner JVs because of the nature of the research question and the additional complexity associated with multiple-partner JVs. After translating the data to English, there were usable responses from 68 JVs. The mean age of the JVs was 4.4 years and the mean number of employees was 330. Note that by using surviving JVs there is a bias towards better performing JVs because, as a JV ages, there is a tendency for either dissolution or takeover. Changes in ownership structure are often precipitated by the dissatisfaction of one or more partners with JV performance.

The analysis examined the relationship between parent ownership and JV performance. Performance was measured using a three-category subjective assessment of performance. Although a single-item indicator of performance is less than ideal, previous research has found that subjective assessments of performance correlate well with objective measures (Geringer and Hebert 1991). Following Blodgett (1992), three categories of JV ownership were used:

1 Majority/minority or minority/majority (highly unequal ownership share).
2 51–49 per cent or 49–51 per cent (somewhat unequal ownership share).
3 50–50 per cent (equal ownership share).

Results

Table 4.1 shows the cross-tabulation of control with performance. The results show no evidence of a relationship between control and performance (chi-square = 7.44, n.s.).

Analysis Two

The second analysis was designed to replicate the relationship examined in Analysis One and also to probe deeper into the control issues. This analysis used the survey of Japanese–North American JVs introduced in the earlier chapters.

Table 4.1 Cross-tabulation of JV performance by Japanese partner
equity (n = 68)

| | JV performance | | | |
	Low	Medium	High	Row total
50–50	3 (6.7)	3 (3.4)	13 (8.9)	19
49%–51%	4 (2.5)	2 (1.2)	1 (3.3)	7
min/maj	17 (14.8)	7 (7.4)	18 (19.8)	42
Column total	24	12	32	68

Chi-square = 7.44,
$p = 0.11$

Note: Numbers in parentheses are expected cell frequencies

The questionnaire measure of performance followed Geringer's and Hebert's (1991) recommendations concerning the validity of subjective questionnaire measures of JV performance. Geringer and Hebert found strong support for using subjective measures of JV performance. The items in the measure were adapted from Geringer and Hebert (1991) and Fornell *et al.* (1990). The questionnaire measure included four items including 'the extent to which the North American partner is satisfied with the performance of the JV' and 'the extent to which the JV has met the objectives for which it was established' (7-point scales; see the Appendix for the complete measure). The Cronbach's alpha for the measure was 0.85. As evidence of the performance measures' convergent validity, the Spearman correlation between the questionnaire measure and the interview classifications discussed in Chapter 2 (treating the classifications as ranks) was 0.75 ($p < 0.001$).

Like the first analysis, JV ownership was used as a mechanism of control. The extent of control used the technique developed by Killing (1983) and replicated by Beamish (1988). Managers were asked to assess the 'jointness' of decision-making regarding ten major decision areas:

- sourcing of raw materials
- product design
- production process
- quality standards
- product pricing
- sales

- the hiring and training of JV managers
- budgeting of sales and cost targets
- capital expenditures
- finance.

Several minor changes were made to Killing's measure. Production scheduling was omitted because it was deemed less important than the others. The sourcing of raw materials as a decision area was added. The control questions were administered in person to the key informants. On the basis of the decision areas, 18 ventures were classified as Japanese partner dominant, 1 as American dominant, 18 as shared management, and 1 as independent of both partners.[4]

To measure control over critical JV resources, the JVs were classified by examining partner management of the JV customer relationship. The customer relationship was used because from both Japanese and American partner perspectives, the JVs were formed primarily to gain access to new customer markets. Therefore, the management of the customer relationship was deemed a critical JV resource. The partner controlling this resource had a source of bargaining power in the JV relationship.

In the JVs where one partner held the dominant share of bargaining power over the customer relationship, this partner was largely responsible for areas such as generating the initial customer contact, negotiating pricing decisions, coordinating product design changes, and managing the sales force. The result of the classification was 25 ventures with Japanese control over the customer relationship, 4 with American partner control, 7 with shared control, and 1 independent.

Results

One-way analysis of variance was used to examine the ownership–performance relationship. Using the three ownership categories used in the first analysis, no significant intergroup differences in performance were found ($F = 0.81$, n.s.).

The decision-based measure of control was used to examine performance in dominant and shared JVs. Because there was only one American partner dominant venture, the two categories of Japanese dominant and shared management ventures were tested. T-test results for these two categories indicated no performance differences (4.29 vs. 4.75, $t = 0.99$, n.s.). No support was found for the argument that JVs with a dominant partner will perform better than ventures where control is shared.

Control from a bargaining power perspective is now examined. The two sets of ventures of American partner dominant customer power and shared customer power were combined into one category. The performance of this group was compared with the performance of the Japanese dominant ventures (i.e. the group with the lower bargaining power from an American partner perspective). The group with greater bargaining power in the critical area of customer relationship management reported higher average performance (5.18 vs. 4.18, $t = 2.55$, $p < 0.05$).[5] Given a predominant JV motive of access to a new product market, a lack of bargaining power associated with customer control seemed to contribute to American parent dissatisfaction with JV performance.

DISCUSSION

From both American and Japanese partner perspectives, no relationship was found between ownership and performance. This suggests that Hamel's (1991) speculation about the relative unimportance of ownership share in the JV process gains some credence. The results from the second analysis suggest that the extent of control may be less important than which partner has the bargaining power in the relationship.

Conceptually, there is a linkage between the extent of control and control over specific activities. Both control dimensions consider JV tasks and partner involvement. However, the extent of control, measured in terms of locus of decision-making, ignores the interplay between JV objectives and control over critical venture activities. When control over critical venture activities is the focus, the associated notion of bargaining power becomes synonymous with control. If JV control is viewed in terms of power and dependence, a single hypothesis about control and performance will not suffice because different types of JVs will involve different distributions of power. In the second analysis, bargaining power was associated with control over the customer relationship. In other JVs, there may be different sources of bargaining power.

A further issue associated with the analysis of control is that JVs, as complex organizational forms, become even more complex to analyse when they are international. Specifically, generalizability across cultures may not be possible. For example, Japanese firms are very effective at using non-ownership control mechanisms in inter-organizational relationships. This can be seen in the Japanese automobile industry, where the vehicle manufacturers each control a network of sub-suppliers through a system of 'vertical contractual dependence' (Turnbull 1989). Thus, studying IJVs without controlling for national culture may not yield useful results.

For managers involved in JVs, an important implication is that in negotiating a JV a firm should focus on how bargaining power will be distributed in the relationship as opposed to partner responsibility for decision-making. If key strategic inputs can be identified and power retained (or at least shared) over these inputs, the question of operational decision-making should be a lesser concern. The second analysis found the American partner firms spending a great deal of time trying to assign responsibility for day-to-day management. Had their focus been on the distribution of bargaining power, JV performance evaluations may have been very different. When a JV is perceived as a blend of both competitive and collaborative goals, increasing bargaining power may lessen dependence on the partner and increase a firm's ability to appropriate value from its JV.

An interesting area for further exploration is the relationship between dependence and the exploitation of JVs as learning vehicles. Hamel (1991) suggested that a firm's dependence within a collaboration may be potentially costly because dependence can inhibit learning (although exploiting a learning opportunity can reduce dependence). Specifically, dependency in a core skill area may disadvantage a firm because it leaves itself open to a partner that is intent on 'stranding' its partner or thwarting the firm's strategic objectives. Hamel found that Japanese firms often were adverse to the notion of symmetrical dependence and preferred alliances with a clearly disproportionate allocation of power. A balance of power was considered unsuitable because it resulted in indeterminateness and instability in the relationship. This finding is consistent with Killing's (1983) argument that because of the difficulties involved with reconciling the often incompatible objectives of the JV partners, dominant control JVs are preferable to shared control ventures.

A related point requiring further research involves the extent to which JVs begin their existence with a liability of newness. This liability may create an unstable bargaining relationship that becomes more stable over time as the partners become familiar with each other and mutual trust increases. As well, the relative importance of JV contributions tends to decrease over time as the JV builds its own culture and systems and gains experience as an entity. It is likely that the JV inputs as determinants of bargaining power lose their importance as the JV ages.

Table 4.2 Views of JV control

	Traditional view of JV control–performance	*View in this chapter*
1 JV objectives	Mutual JV value creation; resources are pooled for cooperative results.	Partner objectives often differ.
2 JV performance	JV can be a success or a failure, individual partner evaluations of performance not considered.	Because partners have different JV objectives, partners evaluate performance independently based on their own value creation objectives.
3 JV control	Control over JV decision-making.	Control over strategic JV resources creates basis for bargaining power (i.e., the partner pulling the key levers has the power).
4 Control– performance relationship	JVs with dominant partners will be more successful; success not clearly defined.	Extent of bargaining power related to partner satisfaction with JV performance.
5 Management implications	Shared decision-making is a recipe for unsuccessful JVs because of partner conflict and disagreements.	Dependent partners will tend to be dissatisfied with JV performance; most JVs are transitional because of unequal bargaining power; shared bargaining power is an elusive concept.
6 Research implications		A global concept of control only captures decision-making and does not isolate bargaining power; also, Killing's view of JV success does not consider unilateral partner views of value creation and performance evaluation.

CONCLUSION

Table 4.2 summarizes the results from this research and how the results challenge Killing's (1983) view of JV control. In particular, the argument is that control over activities creates a dependency perspective and, therefore, a lack of bargaining power in a particular area is potentially a key factor in the evaluation of JV performance. Using the framework developed by Geringer and Hebert (1989), three different conceptualizations of the control–performance relationship were examined. The mixed results support Geringer and Hebert's contention that IJV control is complex and multidimensional. However, the results also raise questions about the degree to which the three control dimensions are, as Geringer and Hebert maintained, interdependent and complementary. Rather than being interdependent, the dimensions may reflect different underlying constructs associated with JV management.

Chapter 5

Collaboration and learning

Conceptual background

The number of IJVs surged through the 1980s and early 1990s. An important explanatory factor for the IJV and strategic alliance trend is the argument that collaboration provides a platform for organization learning, giving partner firms access to the skills and capabilities of their partners (Hamel 1991; Kogut 1988; Westney 1988).

Viewing IJVs as learning opportunities provides an alternative to mutual alliance value creation. IJVs can provide firms with access to the embedded knowledge of other organizations. This access creates the potential for firms to internalize partner skills and capabilities. Huber (1991) referred to this process as grafting, the process by which organizations increase their store of knowledge by internalizing knowledge not previously available within the organization. In an IJV, two or more organizations are brought together because of their complementarity and their differences. The differences in partner skill areas are the fuel for learning. Whether or not the differences are identified and internalized determines whether learning occurs.

While still rather small, there is a growing body of theoretical research (Kogut 1988; Pucik 1991; Westney 1988) and empirical studies (Dodgson 1993; Hamel 1991; Simonin and Helleloid 1993) addressing the issue of IJVs as mechanisms for organizational learning. This stream of research has begun to address some of the important questions associated with how organizations exploit collaborative learning opportunities. Given the premise that IJVs create learning opportunities for the venture partners, this chapter explores the conceptual background associated with learning and collaboration.

LEARNING AND STRATEGY

Organizational learning and the importance of increasing knowledge have long been recognized as having a major impact on a firm's performance. De Geus (1988: 74), for example, suggested that the only competitive advantage the company of the future will have is its managers' ability to learn faster than competitors. Kogut and Zander (1992: 383) argued that theories of the firm should be grounded in the understanding of organizational knowledge. Following these arguments, the position here is that learning and the exploitation of knowledge-based assets are integral elements in the strategic management of an organization.

Traditionally, strategy has been viewed as the match between an organization and its environment (Hofer and Schendel 1986). Works by Chandler (1962), Lawrence and Lorsch (1967), Miles and Snow (1978), and Thompson (1967) established that an organization must align itself with its environment. However, organization–environment fit alone cannot explain firm success (Rumelt *et al.* 1991). An area that is receiving renewed attention is the influence of firm differences in resources on competitive position (see Barney 1991; Mahoney and Pandian 1992). This resource-based view of strategy argues that the origins of competitive advantage are firm resources, which consist of the assets, skills and capabilities, and knowledge controlled by a firm. The configuration and coordination of firm resources determines the degree of non-imitability that is at the heart of competitive advantage. Competitive advantages arise not just through product–market positioning but through the ability to develop new organizational skills.

An important question associated with the resource-based view is how firms augment their range of resources and skills in a changing competitive environment. Organizations can acquire resources in a variety of ways. One, resources can be obtained through factor purchases, such as physical capital and access to raw materials. Two, resources may be the result of a firm's ability to share activities across units. Three, and of primary interest in this study, resources may emerge because of learning through time (Porter 1991). Thus, if the resources of interest are organizational skills that have evolved over time and cannot be purchased in the open market, the role of learning becomes central.

Organizational learning

The term learning refers to the development of skills, knowledge, and associations between past actions, the effectiveness of those actions, and future actions (Fiol and Lyles 1985). The development of skills through a learning process involves the interpretation of past experiences and strategy choices as a basis for present actions (Cohen and Sproull 1991; Porter

1991). The interpretation of experiences involves the processing of information and the generation of knowledge. The knowledge generated through a learning process supports a firm's ability to respond to environmental stimuli and understand the consequences of past actions. The outcome of an effective learning process is reflected in an enhancement of an organization's skills and capabilities (Levinthal 1991).

Despite the logical notion that learning by organizations is essential to their success, there is a lack of synthesis and cumulative work in the area of organizational learning. Ghoshal (1987) maintained that learning as a strategic objective has not been given adequate attention in the strategy literature in general and in the area of global strategies in particular. Mintzberg (1990: 154), an ardent proponent of strategy as a learning process, argued:

> The complex and dynamic nature of the organization's environment, often coupled with the diffusion in the organization of its knowledge base for strategy making, precludes deliberate control; strategy making must above all take the form of a process of learning over time, in which, at the limit, formulation and implementation become indistinguishable. . . . The learning proceeds in emergent fashion through behavior that stimulates thinking retrospectively, so that sense is made of action.

Mintzberg (1990) also suggested that strategic initiatives may be left on their own to develop or flounder or they may be championed by managers higher up in the organization who integrate them with elements of existing strategy. The initiatives create experiences, actions, and strategic choices which provide the basis for learning. The focus of this research is on a particular strategic initiative – the formation of a JV. The JV experience can be the action that 'triggers' learning because it provides new stimuli that may force changes in the mental maps of the organization (Nonaka and Johansson 1985). An underlying assumption is that managers have some understanding of the causal relationships associated with information, action, and outcomes.

LEARNING AND ITS PROCESS ELEMENTS

Learning is closely linked with notions of organizational resources and capabilities. In this section, the process by which various elements converge into coherent organizational action is explored, while recognizing that literature in this area is underdeveloped.

The impetus for the learning process is new information[1] that, from a strategic perspective, is associated with organizational actions (Duncan and Weiss 1979; Huber 1991; Shrivastava 1986). New information originates at the individual level. However, although individuals are the agents of organizational learning, the process involves more than the cumulative learning of individuals. While organizations may not create and store information in the same way as individuals, knowledge and skills are embodied in organizational routines, practices, and cultures (Badaracco 1991). As Hedberg explained with respect to individual versus organizational learning:

> Although organizational learning occurs through individuals, it would be a mistake to conclude that organizational learning is nothing but the cumulative result of their members' learning. Organizations do not have brains, but they have cognitive systems and memories. As individuals develop their personalities, personal habits, and beliefs over time, organizations develop world views and ideologies. Members come and go, and leadership changes, but organizations' memories preserve certain behaviors, mental maps, norms, and values over time. . . . They retain the sediments of past learning after the original learners have left.
>
> (Hedberg 1981: 6)

Similarly, Nelson and Winter, in their seminal work on evolutionary theory, argued:

> To view organizational memory as reducible to individual memories is to overlook or undervalue the linking of those individual memories by shared experiences in the past.
>
> (Nelson and Winter 1982: 105)

Learning begins when an organization interacts with its environment and attempts to discover adaptive opportunities via a search process (Cyert and March 1963). As interactions occur and organizations encounter new experiences, organization members are exposed to various sources of information. The consequences of the environment–organization interactions are the inputs for strategic decision-making (Lenz and Engledow 1986). Through an evaluative process, information perceived as potentially useful for the organization may be acquired by individual managers or organizational sub-units (Huber 1991). Thus, learning by organizations begins in the minds of its managers. Specifically, the cognitive structures of individual managers provide the grounding for organizational learning (Cohen and Levinthal 1990).

Firms acquire information through a variety of formal and informal activities, identified by Huber (1991) as: congenital learning, experiential learning, vicarious learning, searching, and grafting. The processes, although not mutually exclusive, have different conceptual roots and address different aspects of the overall information acquisition process. Of specific interest in this study is grafting, the sub-process by which organizations increase their store of information by internalizing information not previously available; for example, through mergers, acquisitions, and JVs (Huber 1991).

Information perceived as potentially useful for the organization may be acquired by individual managers or organizational sub-units, such as a JV (Huber 1991). New information acquired by an organizational sub-unit has the potential to be shared and distributed within the organization. Through a process of interpretation, the information is given organizational meaning (Daft and Weick 1984). To help explain this cognitive change process, concepts such as frames of reference (Shrivastava and Schneider 1986) and dominant logic (Prahalad and Bettis 1986), have been developed.[2] As individual cognitive structures evolve into shared insights, theories develop about action–outcome relationships between an organization and its environment (Duncan and Weiss 1979).

The outcome of the organizational learning process is considered in detail in the next section. Briefly, when individual learning is integrated into a collective learning base or organizational memory, the stored information from an organization's history can be retrieved and translated into action (Walsh and Ungson 1991). Action is represented by the internalization of managers' experiences into the activities of organizations (Daft and Weick 1984; Nelson and Winter 1982). Thus, for new information to impact organizations strategically, the information must be translated into behaviour or action. The link between organizational information and action and its influence on performance provides the basis for evaluating the effectiveness and 'intelligence' of the organizational learning process.

The learning outcome

By viewing JV value creation through the lens of a learning perspective, the learning outcome becomes a key variable of interest. The outcome of the learning process is the capacity for organizational action. The translation of new knowledge into action is the basis for creating new skills that underpin firm competitive advantage. Thus, as an organization learns, it strengthens and possibly renews its core competence. In turn, core competencies can be seen to represent the collective learning in the organization (Prahalad and Hamel 1990).

The capacity for action, and the capacity for developing core competence, is a function of an organization's skills and capabilities. But what are skills and how are they generated, changed, and enhanced? The concept of organizational routines may help answer this question. Nelson and Winter (1982) developed the concept of routines as an explanation for the persistent features of surviving organizations. They suggested that routines are embedded in an organization and are reflected in an organization's consistency in behaviour.

A review of the literature associated with organizational learning reveals inconsistency in the conceptualization and definition of routines. Various terms have been linked with routines, including policies, techniques, strategy, management practices, programmes, conventions, technologies, structure of beliefs, and habituated action patterns. Porter (1991), drawing on his earlier work on the sources of competitive advantage, suggested that routines represent the intermediate link between firm activities and advantage. A firm is a collection of discrete economic activities; Porter (1985) identified generic categories of activities and classified them as either primary or support activities. Understanding how each activity is performed provides an insight into the behaviour of costs and the existing and potential sources of competitive advantage.

Groups of interrelated activities become organizational routines, of which Winter (1990) identified three distinguishing features. First, routines involve repetitive patterns of activity. Second, they require investment in routine-specific human and physical capital. Third, they have the property of being easily identifiable as patterns of activities and not plans or recipes. The performance of routines creates assets in the form of skills and knowledge. The linkages across an entire firm are captured by the value chain, which is the collection of activities that a firm performs to produce, market, deliver, and support its product (Porter 1985).

The concept of routines is important because it suggests that it is not the discrete activities that are critical to firm success but how they are linked together. Over time, routines may become regular and predictable patterns of activity. Thus, Nelson and Winter (1982: 134) argued, 'As a first approximation . . . firms may be expected to behave in the future according to the routines they have employed in the past.' As routines become practised behaviours, they become the skills and capabilities of a firm and define an organization's capacity for action.

Routines limit and constrain an organization's strategy.[3] However, as Nelson (1991) pointed out, routines do not necessarily imply coherency in firm behaviour. Although a firm may have developed a set of practised routines, strategic choices must still be made. These choices, made under uncertainty about the future, determine how the firm actually competes in the marketplace. For example, a firm may decide to enter a product market for which it has no experience and little knowledge (i.e. no existing routines). Or, established routines may become ineffective when new technologies come into existence. Thus, routines can change, as Winter discussed:

> It is necessary to recognize that routines do change. . . . The patterns of change reflect both the character of environmental pressures and the characteristics of organizations and the routines on which those pressures impinge; the problem is to explain and predict the extent and direction of change under various alternative assumptions regarding the pressures, the organizations, and the routines in place.
> (Winter 1986: 166)

Within a learning framework, the lessons of experience are accumulated in an organization's routines. New experiences may result in the encoding of new lessons into the organizational routines and hence the organization learns. Earlier, organizational learning as more than the sum of individual learning was discussed. Viewing organizations as a set of routines supports that argument because the organization is seen as persisting despite the departure and addition of specific individuals. Consequently, organizational learning becomes more theoretically viable when organizations are viewed as a collection of routines.

An ideal learning experience occurs when a new organizational experience generates collective learning. However, many experiences will not lead to the acquisition of useful knowledge. Or, information will be acquired by individuals or sub-units but not distributed within the organization. Also, as with individuals, learning does not always lead to intelligent behaviour (Levitt and March 1988).

Summary

In concluding this short review of the learning literature, two important points should be noted. First, although no theory or model of organizational learning has gained widespread acceptance, organizational learning is receiving increasing attention from organizational scholars. Literature surveys such as Huber (1991) and Levitt and March (1988) have viewed learning as a fundamental organizational process. Second, that the learning process can be consciously managed, or at least initiated by organizations, is an important assumption in this study. Mintzberg (1990) argued that learning initiatives can occur at various levels of the organization and may be deliberate or accidental. Change associated with a learning process may be proactive if members of the dominant coalition determine when organizational changes are required and what changes can be undertaken (Duncan and Weiss 1979). Thus, while learning may proceed in an emergent fashion, a JV provides a specific initiative that may form the basis for a valuable learning experience. In a sense, managers associated with the initiative may become learning 'champions'. These managers may choose to engage deliberately in learning efforts as a means of gaining access to the skills of the JV partners.

JVs AND LEARNING

An important question is what can be learned from a JV and how might JV-derived knowledge be of strategic use to a parent organization? Learning and the application of JV-derived knowledge can be viewed from three perspectives. First, JV knowledge might be used in the design and management of other JVs and alliances (see Lyles 1988). Simonin and Helleloid (1993) referred to this as collaborative know-how. Second, parent firms may seek access to other firms' knowledge and skills but will not necessarily wish to internalize the knowledge in their own operations. As Hamel (1991) pointed out, knowledge that is embodied only in the specific outputs of the JV has no value outside the narrow terms of the agreement. Thus, a strategic objective of access to a partner's knowledge and skills should not necessarily be equated with a learning objective if new knowledge is to be used solely within the JV entity.

Third, and the focus of this research, knowledge from a JV can be internalized by the parent company to enhance its own strategy and operations. An assumption associated with this use of information is that the knowledge originated with a JV partner.[4] The acquisition of this type of knowledge, called output knowledge by Westney (1988), has been suggested as one of GM's objectives in its JV with Toyota (Keller 1989; Womack 1988). GM hoped to learn about the efficient production of small cars and transfer its knowledge to GM plants. The focus on knowledge useful to the parent is consistent with the identification of learning as a possible motive for the formation of JVs.

Organizations learn through their experiences with both internal and external environments. Badaracco (1991) identified two ideal types of knowledge that help firms to enhance their skills and build sustainable competitive advantages. One type is migratory knowledge, knowledge that can be packaged in a design or manual and can easily migrate from one firm to another. A second type is knowledge embedded in the routines and activities of organizations. Through a JV, the partners may gain access to the organizationally embedded knowledge of other firms. Badaracco described the JV learning challenge:

> When knowledge is embedded, particular problems arise. The knowledge is not available in simple, unitized packages that can be bought for cash. For one organization to secure embedded knowledge from another, its personnel must have direct, intimate, and extensive exposure to the social relationships of the other organization.
>
> (Badaracco 1991: 98)

By definition, organizationally embedded knowledge is difficult to codify and those possessing the knowledge cannot transfer it to others without demonstration and involvement (Pucik 1991; Teece 1984). For example, acquiring the rights to a complex product technology does not guarantee that the necessary information and knowledge are acquired because the most valuable asset, the minds of the innovators, do not accompany the technology (Powell 1987). Because a JV involves co-operative interaction between the partners, the risk that knowledge will dissipate during the transfer may be less than in the case of market-based or contractual transfers of information.

The parent's motives and objectives for collaboration provide the catalyst for learning to occur. Does the parent have a learning objective? Is the formation of the venture motivated strictly by the prospects of improving market position? Will the venture be integrated with parent strategy? The answers to these questions provide an insight into the parent's calculation of potential learning benefits.

Learning stages

With the venture formation, a firm gains exposure to its JV partner and its knowledge base. Information viewed as potentially useful to the parent may be acquired by individuals or sub-units involved in the design and management of the JV. The newly acquired information must then be distributed and interpreted by parent managers for the parent to maximize its benefit from the learning experience. In other words, individual learning must become collective learning. From this perspective, organizational learning in a JV context involves two stages. The two stages are analogous to the innovation diffusion process that also comprises the gathering and transmitting of information across organizational boundaries (e.g. Tushman 1977; Tushman and Scanlon 1981).

The first stage begins with the formation of the JV and partner interactions. The interactions and the managers' exposure to partner knowledge may lead to the recognition of partner skill differences embodied in the JV operation. The nature and extent of managerial interactions and the situational factors surrounding the JV will influence the learning that occurs at this stage. For instance, the perception that a JV partner has inferior technological skills may limit the transfer of technological knowledge.

Using the GM–Toyota JV as an example illustrates the first stage in the learning process. Both GM and Toyota provided managers for the NUMMI JV. GM rotated its managers through the JV and then back to the parent. GM's ability to learn from Toyota initially depended on the extent of the information acquisition by the GM managers with experience in managing the NUMMI venture. According to Keller (1989), the JV managers involved in NUMMI learned a great deal and underwent a 'transformation' in their thinking about the management philosophy of automobile manufacturing.

Information acquired from outside the organization can be used strategically only to the extent that it is distributed and interpreted within the organization (Aguilar 1967; Jelinek 1979). Thus, the second learning stage involves the integration of information acquired by individual managers into the parent's collective knowledge base. This stage involves interaction between the senior managers of the learning organization; namely, the parent managers involved in JV management and those not involved. The input for this stage is the recognition and interpretation of information associated with skill differences between the partners.

What activities must the parent engage in to facilitate the distribution of JV knowledge? Hamel (1991: 84) argued that enhancing the organization's receptivity to learning was a function of the exposure position of the firm *vis-à-vis* its partner. Exposure position involves access to people and facilities. Hamel further suggested that firms would be more successful in exploiting alliance learning opportunities if learning was treated as a rigorous discipline with a focus on the learning task. Thus, the learning firm must engage in activities designed to create a learning awareness at both the JV and parent levels. The firm must also engage in efforts specifically designed to transfer knowledge from the JV to the parent. The parent firm's learning efforts represent the strength or intensity of the learning initiative and provide an indication that the learning process is occurring. In the two-stage model, learning efforts are the critical link between the stages and a key factor in increasing the probability of learning awareness and recognition.

From this perspective, engaging in learning efforts is an indication that learning is occurring and supports the argument by Levitt and March (1988) that learning is a process rather than an outcome. Learning efforts reflect the degree to which the parent is actively trying to internalize the skills and capabilities of its partner. By purposefully engaging in these actions, firms greatly increase the probability that their JVs will contribute to the parent's knowledge base. For example, the rotation of managers through JV positions may encourage the 'bleedthrough' of ideas from the venture to the parent (Harrigan 1985). Hamel (1991) found that firms with a history of cross-functional team-work and inter-business coordination were more likely to transfer JV knowledge to the parent than were firms that emphasized independent business units. Thus, learning efforts provide the mechanism for the JV–parent knowledge transfer.

As a process element, learning efforts can be viewed as both an input and an output of the learning process. As an input, learning efforts provide the mechanism for information to be transferred from the JV to the parent. As an output, learning efforts represent an action that creates an understanding of JV partner capabilities. This perspective is similar to Cohen and Levinthal's (1990) conceptual arguments about the R&D process. They argued that investing in R&D contributes to the genera-tion of a firm's technical knowledge. They observed that R&D creates a capacity to assimilate and exploit new knowledge even though the findings may not lead to specific innovations. They suggested that the knowledge inputs to the innovation process may be as important as the knowledge outputs. Thus, the process involved in generating knowledge may be as important as the outputs from the process because the process ensures that firms develop the deeper understanding necessary to exploit new scientific developments. JV learning efforts can broaden the firm's knowledge base and provide a future basis for effective organizational action. This provides support for the argument that active involvement by JV parents in the learning process can strengthen the learning experience.

Chapter 6

Dimensions shaping the learning process

This chapter begins with a discussion of the learning experience of the American JV parents and their efforts to exploit JV learning opportunities. The chapter then expands on the conceptual background discussion in the previous chapter and empirically examines organizational dimensions that can shape the learning experience. The dimensions examined are:

1 learning capacity;
2 parent experience;
3 partner interactions.

THE LEARNING EXPERIENCE

The automotive supply industry of the early 1990s provided an interesting setting for a study of learning because ongoing structural changes within the industry had effectively created a 'learning imperative' for North American suppliers. Many suppliers found their traditional customer base shrinking. Consequently, access to the Japanese transplant market was seen as a means of maintaining market position. But, to become transplant suppliers, North American firms had to overcome the perception, and perhaps reality, that Japanese suppliers could produce higher quality products at lower prices (Cusumano and Takeishi 1991).

JVs provide companies with a window to their partners' capabilities (Hamel *et al.* 1989). For the American firms in this study, the window had two main sources of potential value. First, all but five JVs were transplant suppliers and, generally, the products supplied to the transplants were similar to products manufactured by the Japanese partners in Japan. The Japanese partners were usually responsible for implementing the manufacturing process, installing the equipment, and supplying the product technology. Consequently, the JVs provided the American partners with a unique opportunity to study a new, state-of-the art organization that would not have been possible without a collaborative relationship.

Second, the JVs were often the American partners' initial experience in supplying Japanese automakers. As a manager explained, Japanese automaker supplier–manufacturer relationships are radically different from those between US auto companies and their suppliers:

> The typical domestic automaker's relationship with its supplier is adversarial. With the transplants, the relationship is supportive if you can deliver the product. Transplants will work with their suppliers and help them when there is a problem. They also expect complete commitment. With our main transplant customer, if there is one problem, there is one phone call; we are expected to fix the problem immediately.

Informants tended to focus on three areas in which the transplants differed from US auto companies in terms of supplier management. One area was pricing practices. The transplants expected that suppliers would meet target prices and that price reductions or cost-downs would occur throughout the model life cycle. In their survey of supplier relationships in the automotive industry, Cusumano and Takeishi (1991) found that prices to the transplants typically decreased annually. In contrast, prices to US automakers rose approximately one per cent annually. The second area of difference was quality management. The transplants expect that parts received from suppliers will be free of defects and, therefore, the burden of parts inspection is pushed down to the supplier level. The third area was the degree of involvement of transplants in supplier operations, as the previous quote indicates.

Most managers believed that the JVs were exceeding the manufacturing capabilities of their American parents. A manager provided an example:

> They [the American partner] are light years behind in terms of their defect rate, their production equipment, their delivery capabilities, etc. They don't have the engineering talent to make changes. To them, manufacturing is a craft. In the JV, the manufacturing process is an engineering process.

This superiority had the potential to create a powerful learning experience for the American partners. The main reasons suggested for the differences in capabilities were the contributions of the Japanese partner and the stringent demands of transplant customers.[1] Indeed, there was only one case where the informant stated that the capabilities of the JV were inferior to those of the American parent.

Learning efforts

Although prior research has discussed the importance of parent involvement in the learning process, few studies have made reference to explicit parent actions. Personnel rotation has been identified as an important parent action (Nonaka and Johansson 1985), and Hamel (1991) made a persuasive argument about the importance of parent involvement in facilitating the internalization of partner skills. Drawing on these references and a series of pilot interviews, learning efforts were measured according to the presence or absence of five broad actions, with the summed score providing a measure of the intensity of learning. These actions were:

1 Rotation of American parent personnel to the JV and back to the parent.
2 Regular visits and tours by parent company executives.
3 Information sharing between the JV and the American parent.
4 Senior American parent management involvement in JV activities.
5 Utilization of the JV relationship to develop closer ties between the American parent and the Japanese parent.

Rotation, regular visits, and information sharing reflect an explicit attempt by the parent to transfer knowledge. Although the latter two actions may not necessarily be put into place with an explicit learning objective, they reflect critical parent activities that should improve the potential for a transfer of knowledge. For the parent management involvement action it is recognized that while operating employees play a vital role in acquiring knowledge, senior management must be committed to the learning process if the parent is to internalize a partner's skills (Hamel *et al.* 1989). The fifth action, utilization of the venture relationship to develop closer ties with the partner, reflects a firm's efforts to gain firsthand access to its partner's operations. For example, several American firms were sending their plant managers to visit the Japanese parent in Japan.

For each learning action, a case was scored as either 1 (occurring) or 0 (not occurring). The actions were summed to yield a score ranging from 0 to 5. As a test of the convergent validity of the learning efforts measure, the scores were correlated with questionnaire responses to the question 'Please indicate the extent to which the North American partner aggressively tries to learn from its JV partner' (7-point scale ranging from 'not at all' to 'to a great extent'). As expected, the Spearman rank-order correlation between learning efforts and the questionnaire response was positive and significant ($r = 0.58, p < 0.001$).

The analysis of learning efforts found that in 30 cases senior American partner management was actively involved in JV management (Table 6.1). Most of the cases with limited senior management involvement were multi-divisional companies in which the JV was a relatively minor operation. Rotation of personnel from the JV to the parent was the learning activity most infrequently used. Both the difficulty of planning for managerial changes and the reluctance of JV managers to move were reasons given to explain the paucity of rotation schemes. For the Japanese partners, rotation schemes were in place for all the JVs.

PARENT LEARNING CAPACITY

Cohen and Levinthal (1990) defined absorptive capacity as the ability to assimilate and exploit new information as the basis for learning. Some organizations, like individuals, may lack the capacity to learn. In the JV context, Hamel (1991) also discussed capacity to learn, arguing that the capacity to learn may be the ultimate source of alliance bargaining power.

Table 6.1 Learning efforts by the American parent

Learning effort	Number of JVs
1 Rotation of managers from the JV to other parent facilities	6
2 Visits and tours of the JV by parent managers	19
3 Shared information between the JV and the parent	24
4 Senior parent management involvement in JV activities	30
5 Parent access to the Japanese partner through the JV relationship	10

Learning intent

Two factors associated with the capacity to learn can be identified. One is the strength of the learning objective. If a learning objective is associated with the formation of a JV, a parent firm may enter more actively into the search for information and encode the information more fully than the firm that is less motivated to learn (Hamel 1991). The presence of a learning objective, or intent, suggests that parent firms recognize the potential learning opportunity. Those firms with an explicit intent should be more likely to engage in learning efforts. As Hamel *et al.* (1989: 138) asserted, 'It is self-evident: to learn, one must want to learn. . . . Western companies must become more receptive [to the benefits of alliance learning].'

When a firm seeks to internalize knowledge from its JV, it can be said to have a learning intent. Hamel (1991: 89-90) defined an alliance learning intent as 'a firm's initial propensity to view collaboration as an opportunity to learn'. Hamel identified several factors contributing to the presence of a learning intent:

1 The parent's view of the alliance as an alternative to competition or as a vehicle for improving competitiveness relative to its partner.
2 The parent's resource position relative to its partner and other firms in the industry.
3 The parent's expected learning benefits.
4 The parent's preference for balanced versus asymmetric dependence within the alliance.

The fourth factor is especially interesting. A firm's dependence within a collaboration may be potentially costly because dependence may inhibit learning. Specifically, dependency in a core skill area may leave a firm open to a partner intent on 'stranding' its partner or thwarting its strategic objectives. Hamel found that Japanese firms often were adverse to the notion of symmetrical dependence and preferred alliances with a clearly disproportionate allocation of power. A balance of power was considered unsuitable because it resulted in indeterminateness and instability in the relationship. This finding is consistent with Killing's (1983) argument that because of the difficulties involved with reconciling the often incompatible objectives of the JV partners, dominant control JVs are preferable to shared control ventures.

Related to the notion of expected learning benefits is the breadth or strength of the learning intent. A narrow learning intent limited to minor aspects of a partner firm's activities may lead a firm in the wrong direction. In the case of NUMMI, GM has been faulted for trying to learn the wrong things (Keller 1989). GM wanted to learn about technological solutions rather than the more subtle, people-oriented practices that characterized Toyota's success. Had GM's learning intent encompassed a broader range of activities, the learning efforts may have been substantially different.

Nevertheless, as the Fuji–Xerox JV vividly illustrates, learning may result despite the absence of an initial learning intent (Jacobson and Hillkirk 1986). The Fuji–Xerox JV was, for the first ten years of its life, strictly a marketing organization. Its mandate was to sell US-made Xerox copiers in Japan. The JV gave Xerox access to Fuji's marketing skills in Japan but, from Xerox's perspective, offered little potential for learning. The choice of the JV mode was motivated by economic and strategic reasons; organizational learning was a minor or non-existent Xerox motivation at the outset. However, the JV subsequently became a significant learning experience for Xerox, contributing skills necessary to compete effectively with Japanese manufacturers in the low end of the copier market.

The study revealed that learning was a JV motive in most cases. Many of the American parents, struggling to compete in an industry in transition, saw their JVs as a point of leverage for the development of new skills and capabilities. Only eight American parents were classified as having no learning intent (for a detailed discussion on the measurement of research variables, see the Appendix). For the strong and moderate intent categories there were 20 and 12 cases respectively. The presence of a strong learning intent seemed to provide the impetus for the initiation of learning efforts. This was supported by the positive relationship between the intent ranks and learning efforts ($r = 0.39, p < 0.01$).[2]

Only one American parent had a learning intent exclusively focused on the Japanese partner's product-based knowledge. This is not surprising given that many supplier firms focus on cost and process improvement. It is also consistent with the argument that the dominant culture of the Japanese firms and its association with technology is generally considered to revolve around manufacturing rather than product design (Burgelman and Rosenbloom 1989).

Strategic centrality

The JV's strategic relationship with its parent is proposed as a second element of learning capacity. The strategic centrality of a JV represents the extent to which managers perceive that a linkage is critical to the strategy of the parent organization (Harrigan and Newman 1990; Shortell and Zajac 1988). Harrigan (1985) discussed parent intervention in the decisions and operations of JVs and suggested that the strongest integration is necessary when the parent hopes to capture internal benefits involving the activities of its ongoing ventures.

Cohen and Levinthal (1990) suggested that effective integration at the learning interface will augment an organization's learning capacity. Thus, a JV perceived as peripheral to the parent organization's strategy will probably yield fewer opportunities for the transfer of JV learning to the parent. A JV viewed as important may receive more attention from the parent organization, leading to substantial parent–JV interaction and a greater commitment of resources to the management of the collaboration. This supports Hamel's (1991) argument that receptivity to learning is enhanced if the parent and its alliance are closely related.

A firm may form a JV with a strong motivation to learn and still consider the JV relatively unimportant to the firm's strategy. This situation could arise if an explicit learning intent is related to limited elements of the parent firm's strategy. GM perceived that learning from Toyota would be confined to production skills in the manufacture of small cars. The GM managers involved in NUMMI soon realized that the lessons to be learned could be applied to the entire parent firm. Managers at the GM head office, however, considered the JV low in importance relative to the overall strategy of the firm and failed to understand the learning potential of the JV (Womack 1988).

Harrigan and Newman (1990) outlined three sources of strategic importance: one, the necessity of the JV to the firm's future activities; two, the urgency of forming the venture – some opportunities must be exploited immediately while others offer a longer planning horizon; and three, the extent to which the venture's activities were interdependent with the parent firm's activities. A JV perceived as unimportant to the parent organization's strategy will probably yield fewer opportunities for the transfer of JV learning to the parent (Hamel, 1991). A JV viewed as important may receive more attention from the parent organization, leading to substantial parent–JV interaction and a greater commitment of resources to the management of the collaboration. Related to importance is the degree of opposition or resistance to a JV. This may play a role in determining how receptive an organization is to new information originating in the JV. High resistance may result in the 'not-invented-here syndrome' and resistance to new information (Shortell and Zajac 1988).

Hamel (1991: 98) found that 'receptivity [to JV learning] seemed to thrive as long as top management continued to express an active interest in what was being learned'. Harrigan (1985) discussed parent intervention in the decisions and operations of JVs and suggested that the strongest integration is necessary when the parent hopes to capture internal benefits involving the activities of its ongoing ventures. New knowledge and skills that are the result of a JV's activities constitute one form of internal benefit for the parent.

The analysis of strategic centrality found a positive correlation between strategic centrality and learning efforts ($r = 0.47$, $p < 0.01$). For several reasons, strategic centrality tended to be high, perhaps even disproportionately high given the JVs' size and contribution to overall parent firm financial results. One, consistent with Harrigan's and Newman's (1990) discussion of JV importance, most of the JVs in the study were related to the parent firms' primary business activities. Two, many American firms viewed transplant market access as critical because of the transplants' increasing market share. Three, the JVs were usually the American partner's first close relationship with a Japanese firm. Since Japanese firms were viewed as a genuine threat to American automotive suppliers, a JV would give the American parent an inside look at the reality of Japanese competition. Finally, the JVs were often the result of an attitude of 'if we can't beat them, join them'. As one executive said, 'The JV was essentially a defensive move. I could not improve the company by myself. I had to find a partner who could help me.'

PARENT EXPERIENCE

In Chapter 5 it was noted that the lessons of experience are incorporated into organizational routines. The learning task itself can be viewed as a specific type of routine. In the JV context, two specific sources of experience were expected to influence the learning process: one, the parent's prior JV experiences and two, the parent's experience with its joint venture partner.

Because there is a learning curve associated with the diffusion of learning (Westney 1988), firms that gain JV management experience may become more efficient at utilizing JVs as learning opportunities. The rationale is that learning may be more difficult in new situations. If firms have a diverse background of experiences, there will be a more robust basis for learning because of the increased probability that incoming information relates to what is already known (Cohen and Levinthal 1990)[3] and is in a form familiar to the parent. Firms that have a base of collaborative experience should have greater knowledge of how to manage, monitor, and appropriate value from their JVs (Simonin and Helleloid 1993), suggesting that JV-experienced firms are more likely to appreciate the learning opportunities created by their JVs. Nevertheless, a contrary argument can be raised. Prior knowledge that has become stable and shared in an organization may interfere with the discovery of contrary experience and new ideas may become lost in the absence of shared interpretation of their meaning (March *et al.* 1991).

The precariousness of new organizations has been discussed extensively in the organizational literature, beginning with Stinchcombe's (1965) arguments about the liability of newness. Stinchcombe suggested that the survival of new organizations is influenced by the strength and duration of personal and interorganizational relationships. When a new JV organization is created, the partners may have initial uncertainties about working together, particularly if they have had no prior interorganizational relationship. On the other hand, new JV relationships that start with an existing stock of 'relationship assets', perhaps via licensing or technology sharing agreements, may begin with a honeymoon period that effectively buffers the firm from early dissolution (Fichman and Levinthal 1991). If firms have worked together in the past, they will have basic understandings about each other's skills and capabilities (Heide and Miner 1992), which should provide an impetus for further learning. As well, experienced partners can forgo the relationship building processes that will be necessary for partners working together for the first time. This indicates that when relationship building has already occurred, learning will be perceived as more tenable because the relationship itself is more likely to be seen as productive. This suggests that prior experience with a JV partner will stimulate learning efforts.

There were 24 cases in which the American parents had prior JV experience and also 24 cases where the partners had been involved in a prior relationship. Neither the experience of having managed a JV nor the experience of having worked with the Japanese partner had a major impact on the learning process. There were no differences in learning efforts between the groups with or without the experience (for JV experience 2.56 vs. 2.00, $t = 1.28$, n.s.; for partner experience 2.28 vs. 2.13, $t = 0.32$, n.s.).

The lack of significant findings for parent experience and learning may be explained by the nature of the JV experiences. These experiences were often very different than anticipated and therefore may have been inadequate in preparing the American partners for their Japanese JVs. Many managers admitted that the American partners were unprepared for their Japanese JV experience and, in particular, unprepared for the rigours of Japanese just-in-time systems and customer demands for flexible production. Shortell and Zajac (1988) found a similar result in their study of internal corporate JVs. They expected a positive relationship between prior experience in related programmes and profitability of a new JV, but instead found a negative relationship. Because the prior experience involved different types of activities than the JV, the learning that occurred from the prior experiences had little transferability to the new JV situation.

Similarly, although a firm may have worked with its partner for many years, the formation of a JV created a new degree of intimacy between the partners. A prior partner relationship may influence the structure of the relationship (e.g. the equity split) and smooth the startup period. However, because the JV establishes a new organization, there are new roles that have to be learned by the two partners. These new roles can be so different from those of prior relationships that the carryover of prior knowledge and its impact on the JV learning experience is limited. An example illustrates that prior partner relationships do not necessarily ensure that the partners understand each other.

> Both partners were naive about the other partner's capabilities and about the nature of the JV. The American partner did not grasp the implications of the changing [automotive] industry structure and how that would impact the JV performance. They did not appreciate the Japanese philosophy. The Japanese partner expected a much leaner partner, one that was prepared to work hard on the JV's behalf. They sensed that management in the American partner was not committed to the same things they were.

PARTNER INTERACTIONS

The third learning dimension is based on the perspective that learning is initiated when organizations interact with their environments and are exposed to various sources of information. In the JV learning context, the environment of interest is the relationship between the partners, and, in particular, the on-going nature of partner interactions. If one partner is to learn from another, the partners must interact and exchange information. As Westney (1988) argued, learning-oriented cooperative strategies involve a denser and more varied set of interorganizational interactions relative to output-oriented strategies. Partner interactions may range from operational information exchanges necessary to run the JV to the sharing of more strategic information.

Given that JVs are voluntary interorganizational relationships, a social exchange approach with its emphasis on purposeful coordination

(Schmidt and Kochan 1977) can provide a basis for examining the interactions. The behavioural factors associated with transactions between two or more parties are the focus of social exchange. In an organizational setting, the exchange perspective is characterized by an emphasis on interfirm interactions and non-economic outputs from the relationship (Dwyer *et al.* 1987).

Two exchange factors are proposed as critical to the learning process. The first, trust between JV partners, has been identified as an important element of long-term JV relationships (Beamish 1988; Harrigan 1986; Sullivan and Peterson 1982). Breakdowns in the value creation process in JVs often stem from a lack of trust between partners (Borys and Jemison 1989). Trust reflects the belief that a partner's word or promise is reliable and that a partner will fulfil its obligations in the relationship. An atmosphere of trust should contribute to the free exchange of information between committed exchange partners since the decision-makers do not feel that they have to protect themselves from the others' opportunistic behaviour (Blau 1964; Jarillo 1988). Without trust, information exchanged may be low in accuracy, comprehensiveness, and timeliness (Zand 1972).

The second exchange variable is relationship openness. In a truly cooperative JV, extensive communication between the partners is an essential feature of the relationship. The quality of inter-partner communications reflects the formal and informal sharing of meaningful and timely information (Anderson and Narus 1990; Hall *et al.* 1977). Gupta (1987) examined openness in the relationship between corporate and business unit managers. Openness reflected the degree to which relations between business unit managers and their corporate superiors are open and informal and allow for spontaneous and open exchange of information and ideas (Gupta 1987).

In the alliance context, relationship openness can be defined as the willingness and ability of the JV partners to share information and communicate openly. Hamel (1991: 94) defined openness and accessibility of JV partners as transparency. Four determinants of partner transparency were identified:

1 The penetrability of the social context surrounding the partner.
2 Attitudes towards outsiders, i.e. clannishness.
3 The extent to which the partner's distinctive skills were encodable and distinct.
4 The partner's relative pace of skill-building.

Hamel argued that openness between collaborative partners was an essential element in the learning process. This suggests that parent firms that view their JV relationships as open are more likely to invest resources in learning. Hamel also found that some organizations were more penetrable than others and systematic asymmetries in openness existed between Western and Japanese partners. These asymmetries had the potential to influence the learning process.

In this study, relationship openness reflects the willingness and ability of the JV partners to share information and communicate openly. A firm may wish to restrict its flow of knowledge to the JV for various reasons, including a desire to maintain its influence over the other partner(s) (Hamel *et al.* 1989). In the case of international JVs, openness may be a function of cultural or language differences (Kanter 1989) and access to facilities of the partner (Hamel 1991). Openness also may be closely related to the degree of trust that the partner has in the JV relationship because, in the absence of trust, the partner is unlikely to share information.

The nature of the partner interactions, and in particular trust and openness between the partners, was expected to create an environment that facilitated exchange. Trust was identified by many informants as a significant predictor of JV performance. Trust was also suggested as a major factor in Japanese firms' selection of a JV partner and, possibly, the most important factor. However, the role of trust in the learning process was difficult to establish. While there was a positive relationship between trust and learning efforts ($r = 0.35$, $p < 0.05$), the different American and Japanese attitudes toward trust raise questions about dimensionality of the concept. As Parkhe (1993) suggested, trust may be a core concept in international JV research but because of its 'messy' nature, it has remained beyond the grasp of researchers (see Chapter 3 for a more complete discussion of JV trust).

The openness of the relationship was suggested as an important factor in stimulating parent learning efforts and influencing the availability of transferable JV knowledge. The relationship between openness and learning efforts ($r = 0.39$, $p < 0.05$) suggests that openness plays a role in the initiation of the learning process. If a JV relationship is perceived as open and the partner is willing to share information, parent firms may consider it worthwhile to initiate learning efforts.

Informants usually described the JV and their Japanese partner as open, although when the ventures were outside the American parent's main product strategy, the Japanese partner tended to be more open than when the venture manufactured a product similar to the American parent.[4] It is likely that the Japanese partners in these new product ventures were more open because they felt that an American partner learning strategy was not a serious competitive threat. A firm may wish to restrict its flow of knowledge to the JV if the partner is perceived as a potential competitor (Hamel *et al.* 1989).

Openness was also generally described as if it were a function of the Japanese partner's willingness to share information rather than a mutual sharing of information between the partners. The general view was that the Japanese partners controlled the most valuable information in the JV. Therefore, although openness is a JV variable, it was oriented toward the American partner's view of its Japanese partner's willingness to share information. This finding is consistent with Hamel's (1991) assertion that Western alliance managers generally believed that the Western firms were more open than their Japanese partners. In this study, American managers almost took it as a given that the American firm would share information with its Japanese partner. That the Japanese partner was also willing to share information was viewed as somewhat surprising by many managers.

CONCLUSION

This chapter and the findings discussed support the premise that JVs create learning opportunities for the JV parents. Consistent with the conceptual arguments of various scholars, JVs provide substantial opportunities for firms not only to gain access to partner skills, but more importantly to internalize those skills.

In general, the results are supportive of prior research. There are, however, several important differences and extensions in the current study. First, this study narrowed the research focus to a single industry and a specific type of alliance, equity JVs. Controlling for industry and alliance type and the partner's country of origin was necessary given the complexity of alliances and the limited research on collaboration and learning. Also, it allowed for a more in-depth examination of the contextual environment in which learning occurs. Second, this study probed the basic issue of learning as a viable JV objective. Evidence was found to support the argument that JVs create exploitable learning opportunities. Third, attention was focused on explicit firm learning experiences and the efforts undertaken to exploit learning opportunities. Fourth, the multimethod approach allowed for a refinement in the theoretical orientation of the framework concepts.

The establishment of the learning intent

A strong learning intent is an essential aspect of a firm's learning capacity and can provide the catalyst for learning efforts. However, the learning intent must be realistic and consistent with partner capabilities. If the learning intent and the assessment of learning potential are unrealistic, there may be misplaced expectations about the explicitness or discreteness of partner skills and the ease of knowledge transfer. Thus, it is not enough to want to learn; firms must also understand their partners and the substance of the learning opportunity.

It emerged that the American firms often had a preconceived assessment of Japanese skills and capabilities. This assessment contributed to the strength of the learning intent and was often rooted in a belief that Japanese manufacturing was innately superior to North American manufacturing. The next chapter explores this issue in more detail by examining how managerial beliefs associated with an unwillingness to cast off or unlearn past practices can severely limit the effectiveness of organization learning.

Chapter 7

A multi-level framework of organizational learning

This chapter was co-authored by Mary M. Crossan

This chapter builds on the earlier conceptual discussion. Some of the more controversial areas in the organizational learning literature are examined as the basis for developing a multi-level learning framework and applying it to the JV context. The framework provides the underpinnings for an important argument: that an existing set of managerial beliefs can constrain the learning process and hence the notion that 'I'll see it when I believe it' rather than 'I'll believe it when I see it'.[1] The latter view is based on an information processing perspective of learning, while the former is based on an interpretive perspective. This distinction may be the primary reason that researchers underestimate the complexity of organizational learning. It is often assumed that once managers are exposed to a new idea or technology, learning will occur. We observed firms with explicit learning objectives struggling to capitalize on their JV learning opportunities. While individual managers in the JVs were often enthusiastic and positive about their learning experiences, integration of the learning experience at the parent firm level was problematic. The fundamental position in this chapter is that a rigid set of managerial beliefs associated with an unwillingness to cast off or unlearn past practices can severely limit the effectiveness of organizational learning.

A LEARNING FRAMEWORK

In our view, the major areas of disagreement among organizational learning theorists are:

1 whether organizational learning occurs at the individual, group, or organization level;
2 whether learning refers to cognitive and/or behavioural change and how the two are related;

Table 7.1 Learning in organizations

Level	Process	Outcome
Individual	Interpreting	Schema, cognitive map
Group	Integrating	Shared belief structures
Organization	Institutionalizing	Structure, systems, organization context

3 whether learning refers to content or process;
4 whether learning should be tied to performance.

The organizational learning framework in Table 7.1 suggests that learning in organizations:

1 occurs over three levels – individual, group, and organization;
2 involves both behavioural and cognitive change;
3 involves a process of change in cognition and behaviour where the changes may be viewed as the outputs or content of learning;
4 should not be tied directly to performance enhancement.

After providing an overview of these four elements, we apply the framework to the JV study.

Levels of learning: individual, group, organization

Perhaps one of the weakest links in current theories of organizational learning is failure to take a multi-level perspective. Since learning occurs through individuals, it is necessary to have a grasp of individual learning before adding the complexity of the organization setting. We suggest that a concept of individual learning should be embedded in a concept of group learning, which in turn should be embedded in a concept of organizational learning. At each level of learning, different learning processes are at work, as shown in Table 7.1. At the individual level, the critical process is interpreting; at the group level, integrating; and at the organization level, institutionalizing. This perspective of learning is similar to Nonaka's (1994) notion of knowledge creation as an upward spiral process, starting at the individual level, moving up to the group level, and then to the organizational level. The outcome or product of the individual process of interpreting is a change in individual beliefs or schemas and individual behaviours. The manifestation of this product is individual behaviours. The product of the group process, manifested in coordinated group actions, is shared beliefs and concerted actions. The product of the organization process is the institutionalization of an organization schema reflected in the organizational systems and routines (March 1991; Starbuck 1983). The manifestation of institutionalization outcomes is organizational strategy as reflected by a coherent pattern of actions.

The relationship between cognition and behaviour

Discussions of individual learning generally refer to the product of the learning process as changes in beliefs (or cognition) and changes in behaviour. The term skill is often used to describe behaviours for which an individual has developed a level of expertise or proficiency. While individual learning theorists continue to debate the relative merits of cognition over behaviour (Mazur 1990), we argue that cognition and behaviour are so tightly intertwined that it is counter-productive to define learning as change in either one or the other. Rather than describing learning as a particular state of cognitive or behavioural change, different types of learning will depend on whether there is cognitive and/or behavioural change, as shown in Figure 7.1. Since individual learning is the foundation of organizational learning, the learning states are introduced with reference to individuals. Subsequently, the individual learning states will be extended to the organization level.

Clearly, in cases of no cognitive or behavioural change, there is no learning. Conversely, when both changes occur, the outcome is integrated learning, as shown in Figure 7.1. This chapter suggests that change in behaviour without a corresponding change in cognition, or change in cognition without a corresponding change in behaviour, are transitional states since they create a tension between one's beliefs and one's actions. The tension, however, is a cognitive tension between the interpretation of one's behaviours and other beliefs. This tension is synonymous with the concept of cognitive dissonance. Festinger (1957: 4) supported the argument that the tension is transitional, stating that 'the reduction of dissonance is a basic process in humans'.

Changes in behaviour without any change in cognition may be resolved in several ways. If the behavioural change arises from forced learning it will probably resolve itself into the no-learning quadrant. Individuals will continue to interpret stimuli through their current belief systems, reinforcing existing beliefs. For example, individuals who feel

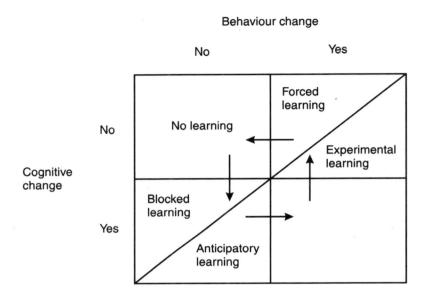

Figure 7.1 The relationship between cognition and behaviour

forced to comply with governmental environmental standards may change their behaviours to comply with the standards. In doing so, they reinforce their views that government should not be intervening in their affairs. However, if the learning is experimental, individuals may try new behaviours that result in cognitive change. There may then be a shift into the integrated learning quadrant. A key aspect of experimental learning is that individuals are willing to suspend their belief systems to try a new behaviour, and in doing so are open to new and different interpretations of the results of the behaviour.

Although a transitional state of behavioural change not accompanied by cognitive change may be resolved, a cautionary point should be raised. The model is designed to provide insight into the relationships between cognition and behaviour, as opposed to a definitive statement about how and why the change occurs. As evidence of the complexity of the cognition–behaviour debate, Schein (1971), for example, devoted an entire book to describing how and why American civilians held by the Chinese communists between 1950 and 1956 changed or failed to change their beliefs as a result of the treatment they received.

A third transitional state occurs when individuals experience cognitive change without any behavioural change. In the simplest case, called anticipatory learning, a gap occurs between a change in cognition and the display of a change in behaviour. For example, many years of medical education are required before a physician can attempt the first operation. Nonetheless, it is the changes in cognition arising from the medical education which guide the surgeon in the behaviour required to perform the operation.

The more difficult cases are those in which individuals have undergone changes in cognition that are not reflected in their behaviour and may probably never be reflected in their behaviour. This situation is often associated with a physical skill such as playing golf or running. Although individuals may have experienced changes in cognition so that they 'know' what they are supposed to do, they are not able to execute that know-how. In fact, they may not possess the physical resources to translate the know-how into action.

There are other cases where a change in cognition does not lead to a change in behaviour. Blocked learning occurs when other beliefs override the situation. For example: I know the customer is always right, but I can't take this kind of abuse. To see the learning manifested in behaviour, it is necessary to deal with the blocking element. For example, customer representatives might treat customers better if they did not have to deal with the extreme abuse they received from customers irate over shoddy products or service.

The debate in the psychology literature between learning as cognitive change and learning as behavioural change is also a point of contention for organizational learning theorists. For example, Fiol and Lyles (1985) distinguished between cognitive change and behavioural change by suggesting that cognitive change is learning and behavioural change is adaptation. Firms in mature industries with stable environments were characterized as having low levels of cognitive or behavioural changes. These firms would be classified in the no-learning quadrant in Figure 7.1. Fiol and Lyles suggested that organizations in crisis or undergoing rapid restructuring, perhaps through mergers, are characterized by a high level of behavioural change with a low level of cognitive change. By extending the previously discussed learning categories to an organization level, this type of transitional stage is similar to the forced learning and experimental learning situations shown in Figure 7.1. Friedlander (1984) supported the concept of forced learning, suggesting that mandated policy changes, for example, lead to changes in organization behaviour but not to changes in organization cognition.

Researchers have also argued that learning is contingent upon the turbulence of the environment. Firms in industries experiencing structural change may be under pressure to learn new skills and capabilities (Kogut 1988). Fiol and Lyles (1985) characterized organizations with a low level of behavioural change and a high level of cognitive change as being in a turbulent environment where too much change could cause the organization to lose its sense of direction. However, we suggest that it may be a matter of timing for the behavioural change, as opposed to overt resistance to change. The behavioural change may occur but only after a time lag. Fiol and Lyles also suggested that a high level of cognitive and behavioural change is appropriate for organizations in a moderately turbulent environment. We suggest that this type of integrated learning will be a source of competitive advantage for organizations and therefore should be viewed as an ideal state.

The issue of whether organizational learning encompasses cognitive change, behavioural change or both is not a trivial matter. The definition which theorists adopt becomes the belief system that, in essence, guides their discoveries about the phenomenon of organizational learning. Our position is that defining organizational learning as involving either cognitive or behavioural change unnecessarily narrows the perspective of organizational learning. Furthermore, in an effort to distinguish between the two types of change, theorists may fail to recognize and investigate the important linkages between the two. As Gioia and Manz asserted (1985: 527), 'although a great deal of energy has been spent debating the issue of cognition versus behaviour, less effort has been devoted to the study of the more important issue of the connection between cognition and behaviour'.

Learning process and content

Underlying the learning framework in Table 7.1 is a set of assumptions about the process of learning. Changes in both cognition and behaviour have been highlighted as the products or outcome of the learning process. Many theorists focus on these content aspects of learning without delving further into the process. We suggest that the process of organizational learning should be conceived of as a dynamic interplay among beliefs, behaviours and stimuli from the environment, where beliefs are both an input and a product of the process as they undergo change.

At the core of learning is a process that involves (1) the detection of a mismatch between one's beliefs and perceptions of stimuli and (2) the modification of beliefs to resolve the mismatch. A mismatch, or discrepancy, may be experienced as a gap, for which the individual has no expectations of a particular stimulus, or as a conflict between expectations and actual experiences. Weick (1979) used the term enactment to define the stimulus encounter, describing it as 'the bracketing of some portion of a stream of experience for further attention'. A second process, selection, involves the interpretation of experiences, and retention refers to the storage of the interpretation as a guide for further applications.

While a primary reason for not processing stimuli is not noting them, a primary reason for not noting stimuli is a belief system that directs attention in a different direction.

> There is a dialectical contradiction between these two requirements: we cannot perceive unless we anticipate but we must not see only what we anticipate.... Although a perceiver always has at least some (more or less specific) anticipation before he begins to pick up information about a given object, they can be corrected as well as sharpened in the course of looking.... The upshot of the argument is that perception is directed by expectations but not controlled by them.
>
> (Neisser 1976: 43)

Neisser's comments demonstrate how beliefs both guide and are a product of the learning process. Although beliefs guide what is enacted and interpreted, Neisser suggested that they do not control the process. Thus, there is the opportunity to interpret stimuli that may alter one's beliefs.

As an input to the process of learning, a highly developed belief system with many concepts and interrelationships enables an individual to make subtle distinctions and notice differences others may miss. Neisser used the example of a chess master to illustrate how the expert's ability to discriminate differed from that of the novice:

> The information that the master picks up from the chessboard determines not only where he will move his pieces but where he will move his eyes. Observations show that a good chess player's eye movements are closely related to the structure of the position on the board; he looks at crucial pieces and crucial squares. He quite literally sees the position differently – more adequately and comprehensively – than a novice or a nonplayer would. Of course, even the nonplayer sees a great deal: the chessmen are of carved ivory, the knight resembles a horse, the pieces are (perhaps) arrayed with a certain geometrical regularity. The differences among these perceivers are not matters of truth and error but of noticing more rather than less.

The information that specifies the proper move is available in the light sampled by the baby as by the master, but only the master is equipped to pick it up.

(Neisser 1976: 181)

In summary, the debate on the relationship between cognitive change and behavioural change has tended to focus on the products of the learning process rather than on the process of learning. This chapter suggests that the process of organizational learning must be integrated with the learning product or outcome. As indicated earlier, the process involves three levels: interpreting, integrating, and institutionalizing. Individual beliefs guide the process through the identification of gaps and conflicts, and are a product of the process as gaps and conflicts are resolved.

Learning and performance

The relationship between organizational learning and performance has generated a great deal of controversy in the field of management. Some theorists have equated learning with performance enhancement (Argyris and Schon 1978; Fiol and Lyles 1985; Gronhaug 1977), while others have distinguished between the two. Our position is that organizations that learn more effectively will, in the long run, perform better than their competitors. However, while there should be a link between organizational learning and performance, time lags between the two make empirical observations very difficult. Additionally, organizations can incorrectly learn and they can correctly learn that which is incorrect (Huber 1991).

March *et al.* (1991) addressed a similar issue in their discussion of reliable and valid learning. They suggested that in a reliable learning process, an organization develops common understandings of its experience and makes its interpretations public, stable, and shared. In a valid learning process, an organization understands, predicts, and controls its environment. As organizations engage in learning efforts, neither reliability nor validity is assured because different people and groups in an organization approach historical experience with different expectations and beliefs. As we found, shared understanding about the value of JV learning experiences was often obstructed by the variety and differences in managerial beliefs.

March (1991) also qualified the relationship between learning and performance. March argued that although learning is a major component in any effort to improve organizational performance and strengthen competitive advantage, the increased knowledge associated with a learning process may reduce the variability of performance rather than increase it. In that sense, learning makes performance more reliable. The risk associated with reduced variability is that the organization may become resistant to contradictory information.

Thus, performance provides important feedback about the efficiency and effectiveness of a learning process and, ultimately, an organization's strategy will come to reflect the accumulated learning (Mintzberg 1990). However, to suggest that incremental learning should always lead to incremental performance improvements is misleading. Specific performance enhancements may result because of learning but they also may be attributable to efforts of imitation, regeneration, or technological development. More important, learning and the learning benefits may be separated in time, or the benefits may be masked by intervening forces.

Summary

The three levels of learning presented in Table 7.1, and the associated processes and outcomes provide a framework with which to examine learning in organizations. For each element of the framework there is a potential tension that is either a supporting or limiting factor in an organization's ability to capitalize fully on learning opportunities. For example, at the individual level, how does an individual's schema affect the process of interpreting? What is the relationship between cognition and behaviour? At the group level, what is the relationship between the learning process and the learning product? How is learning shared across group and organization boundaries? How does group learning become institutionalized into the organizational routines? What are the performance implications associated with the learning products at each of the three levels? Clearly, for an individual experience to become institutionalized in organizational systems and routines, there are many hurdles to overcome.

By delineating the different levels involved in the organizational learning process, empirical research can be more focused and, hopefully, generate new insights. The framework presented in Table 7.1 can be used to highlight the factors that influence learning at the individual, group and organization levels. In the next section we use the organizational learning framework as a lens to examine JV learning.

THE FRAMEWORK APPLIED TO JV LEARNING

As discussed in Chapter 6, the American partner usually gained the equivalent of unhindered access to the dedicated assets of their Japanese partners. Despite this access, learning often proved to be a difficult experience for American managers and their firms. Applying the learning framework to the data provides insight into the learning process. The following discussion is organized into four sections. The first three relate to learning at each of the levels identified in Table 7.1: individual, group and organization. Observations about the relationship between cognition and behaviour, and learning as a process, are incorporated into the discussion of the learning levels. The fourth section addresses the relationship between learning and performance.

Individual learning: changes in managerial cognition and behaviour

The data suggest that at the managerial level in the American firms, existing sets of beliefs severely constrained the learning process. American managers often failed to understand or appreciate their Japanese partner's areas of competency. A common expectation was that the knowledge associated with differences in skills between the Japanese and American partners would be visible and easily transferrable. However, as Kogut and Zander (1992) pointed out, knowledge can be classified as information or know-how. Information implies knowing what something means and know-how is a description of knowing how to do something. Information is lower-level knowledge and far more accessible to outsiders. The American parent firms focused their learning efforts on visible information and differences rather than on partner know-how, an obstacle that has plagued General Motors in its JV with Toyota (Keller 1989).

The notion of visible differences is analogous to Badaracco's (1991) description of migratory knowledge. Migratory knowledge was defined as knowledge that can be clearly and fully articulated and, therefore, is very mobile. Many American firms in this study expected to find migratory knowledge that could be transferred on a piecemeal basis. Instead, they encountered differences that were embedded in the know-how of their partners. Thus, the learning opportunities associated with the Japanese firms were generally not product- or technology-specific but related to an overall philosophy of doing business. An executive described an American firm's learning situation:

The American partner initially thought that access to the Japanese partner's manufacturing technology would be very important and that they would learn a lot about their partner's operation. However, the expectations were very general and were not in sharp focus. Once the JV relationship was formed and the American partner had the opportunity to see its partner's operation, they were subtly surprised by the simplicity of things. The key difference was improvement for improvement's sake and not sophisticated technology differences. The main differences were simple things like always paying your suppliers on time and shipping 7200 parts not 7201. . . . I was surprised by the simplicity of the differences between the two partners and so was the American partner CEO.

The dilemma facing American firms is described by an executive:

Most companies enter a JV [with a Japanese partner] expecting to find visible differences that are not only unique but unknown to the rest of the industry. The reality is that the differences will be unique but they will be subtle. The differences are also going to be managerial rather than technological. That may require an admission that American managerial practice may be part of the problem. Many managers find that hard to admit.

While the complexity of a manager's beliefs or schema could facilitate the identification of the subtle differences between Japanese and American operations, hands-on, original experience is usually the catalyst in knowledge creation (Nonaka 1994). Hence, behavioural change often preceded cognitive change. The differences, such as 7,200 parts not 7,201 parts, were visible and easily recognized, but the deeper meaning associated with the differences required hands-on experience. American managers not involved in the JV management or its operation did not have the direct experience and, therefore, may not have appreciated the deeper meaning. These managers saw the flow of information concerning quality differences and delivery capabilities. However, information in the absence of the expertise and know-how behind the information is insufficient to effect cognitive change (Starbuck 1992).

When there were clearly identified performance benefits managers were more willing to engage in experimental learning. In an experimental situation, managers try out new behaviours even though they may not have fully understood or agreed with them. In cases where performance benefits were not clearly identifiable, managers were reluctant to experiment. One manager suggested that North Americans tend to look for 'home runs' before changes will be considered, consistent with the view that Western organizations learn in large, discrete steps (Hedlund and Nonaka 1993). This proved problematic, since much of what was to be learned from the JVs was of an incremental nature. Those managers recognizing partner differences as incremental, managerial and inextricably linked to their Japanese partner's business philosophy were usually more successful in their learning efforts.

In summary, we observed that the individual process of interpreting was affected by the complexity of managerial schemas, the managers' hands-on exposure to the activities of the Japanese partner, and managers' appreciation of the subtle differences that may not be directly tied to performance enhancement.

The sharing and integration of managerial learning

Individual knowledge and perspectives remain personal unless they are amplified and articulated through social interaction (Nonaka 1994). The data suggest that the process of integrating individual learning into collective or shared learning was a major organizational challenge. Managers at the JV level were often frustrated by the apparent inability of the American parents to go beyond recognition of potential learning experiences to exploitation of the experiences. For example, a manager commented:

> The American parent should be learning through this experience. What good is the JV if the people and information in the JV do not go back to the parent? This information should not be limited to the partnership.

Three types of mechanisms can promote individual to collective integration:

1 Personal facilitation where a leader or influential individual guides the integration of the various schemas to develop a shared understanding.
2 Shared facilitation where the individuals involved share enough common ground, or have enough trust and respect, to manage the integrating process themselves.
3 Artifactual facilitation where the organization's systems and structures act as integrating mechanisms.

In the case of JVs, where managerial learning in the venture must migrate to a higher organizational level in order to impact the parent, integration through organizational artifacts can occur through various avenues. These avenues, discussed in Chapter 6 as learning efforts, include:

1 The rotation of managers from the JV back to the parent; regular meetings between JV and parent management.
2 JV plant visits and tours by parent managers.
3 Senior management involvement in JV activities.
4 The sharing of information between the JV and the parent.

Each of these avenues involves links between individuals that span boundaries.

The integration of individual learning across boundaries provides the basis for Brown and Duguid's (1991) concept of evolving communities of practice. Communities emerge not when the learners absorb abstract knowledge but when the learners become 'insiders' and acquire the particular community's subjective viewpoint and learn to speak its language. In several cases, JV managers referred to parent managers as 'transformed' because the parent and JV managers both saw the learning potential in the JVs. From Brown and Duguid's (1991) perspective, a community of practice had emerged.

While there may be organizational mechanisms in place that have the potential to facilitate integration, other factors inhibited the integrating process. We observed that some parent company managers were threatened by the learning occurring in the JV. This contributed to a situation of blocked learning, with managers discounting much of what was occurring in the JV. For example, the parents may have had difficulty accepting the JV child, a new organization with limited experience, as a legitimate 'teacher'. As a JV general manager explained:

> Yes, they [American parent management] know that there are differences [in the JV and originating with the Japanese partner] but it is difficult for them to internalize the reasons for the differences. At a high level in the parent organization, people should be in a position to look at the JV and at the parent operations to see the differences and learn from the JV experience. But, you have to understand the people involved. It is very difficult for them to openly discuss the situation, particularly when it is the child that is outperforming its parent.

Managers in the American parents were often willing to concede that their partners were capable of producing a superior product. However, a focus on the key to the Japanese 'mystique' was inevitably futile. A manager explained:

We [American partner management] initially thought that access to the Japanese partner's manufacturing technology would be very important and that we would learn a lot about their operation. However, the expectations were very general and were not in sharp focus. Once the JV relationship was formed and we had the opportunity to see their operation, we were subtly surprised by the simplicity of things. The key difference was improvement for improvement's sake and not sophisticated technology differences.

Another JV executive described the inability of the American partner to make sense of its JV:

The American partner is in a different business than the Japanese partner. They are in the commodity business. Machines are run until they wear out. There is no capital reinvested. The Japanese partner is in a dynamic business in which capital must be reinvested to compete. There is always pressure to lower costs and to improve the product. It's hard for them [the American partner] to understand the JV business. They would have liked to get involved with the JV but they don't understand what the JV does.

This example illustrates a situation in which the parent managers, possibly because they did not experience the JV on a firsthand basis, seemed to lack the appropriate context for exploiting the learning opportunity. The JV manager was convinced of the validity of the learning opportunity. Unfortunately, the parent managers were unable to discard an existing belief system and recognize the learning and competitive implications associated with the JV. Consequently, integration into shared belief structures did not occur.

A related point, suggested by Hamel (1991), is that American firm reluctance to engage in experimental learning was associated with the perspective of the JV role. The JVs were often seen as stand-alone operations utilizing a set of complementary skills, rather than a bridge to the development of new skills in the parent (this point is considered in more detail in Chapter 10). If JVs are viewed as a means of skills substitution rather than skills enhancement, learning will not be seen as a high priority. A focus on skills enhancement requires a willingness to suspend an existing belief system in favor of new behaviour.

Finally, we found that in several cases, parent managers recognized the value of the learning opportunity when the degree of skill discrepancies between the JV partners became too great to ignore. An executive described the situation at the American parent after a skills gap was identified:

Initially, we thought there was nothing to learn from our partner. We thought we were better than anybody. When we first went to Japan we thought our partners wanted a JV so they could learn from us. We were shocked at what we saw on that first visit. We were amazed that they were even close to us, let alone much better. We realized that our production capabilities were nothing [compared with the Japanese firm's]. We realized that we were not world class. Our partner was doing many things that we couldn't do.

In summary, our observations suggest a strong need for leader and artifactual facilitation to overcome the barriers to shared integration. Unfortunately, many companies were unwilling to incur the minimal expense of setting up learning-oriented systems, such as sending key parent managers to the JV on a regular basis to experience the JV firsthand. This type of action may have been seen as wasteful and not directly associated with successful JV management. However, as Nonaka (1990) suggested, allowing individuals to enter each others' areas of operation promotes the sharing and articulating of individual knowledge, which may lead to problem generation and knowledge creation. Nonaka referred to the outcome of this conscious overlapping of company information and business activities as redundancy of information. Our observations suggest that the Japanese parents frequently took the opportunity to send their Japan-based managers to visit the JV, probably because of a greater tolerance for redundancy and because in Japanese firms life-long learning is an explicit element in the career path of Japanese managers (Hedlund and Nonaka 1993; Keys *et al.* 1994).

Learning at the organization level

The majority of JVs had been operating for five to six years. While there was evidence of institutionalized learning, there was far less than one might expect given the potential for learning that existed. To explain the dearth of organizational level learning, we propose that as individual learning spirals its way to the organization level, dissipation in learning will occur. The rate of dissipation will be influenced by a variety of factors. Successful firms may become increasingly narrow in their perspective (Miller 1993) and committed to a particular strategy. When confronted with learning opportunities, successful firms may see little need to change behaviour and, thus, become trapped by their distinctive competence (Levinthal and March 1993). The strength of a firm's learning intent will help to determine the organizational resources committed to learning (Hamel 1991). The type of institutional learning mechanisms plays a key role in how new knowledge is 'managed' by JV parent firms (Hedlund and Nonaka 1993). Finally, the nature of managerial belief systems permeates all levels of learning and, correspondingly, contributes to learning dissipation.

As the learning process takes place and as the individual to group integration occurs (or does not occur), pieces of knowledge and information disappear. This dissipation means that, in reality, new knowledge and ideas at the managerial level have a low probability of becoming institutionalized learning. The JV study showed that rather than using institutional mechanisms to transfer learning throughout the organization, learning was often transferred from group to group on an ad hoc and informal basis. Again, given the barriers to group and organization integration, dissipation of the learning was likely to occur.

Learning and performance

The relationship between learning and performance at an organizational level was interesting. Managers in the American parent companies frequently pointed to the poor financial performance of the JVs as evidence that learning was not occurring, or could not occur.[2] The Japanese parents, on the other hand, generally had longer time horizons and different expectations regarding JV performance. Informants indicated that the American JV partners were more likely than the Japanese to use profitability as a measure of both learning and JV success. A JV manager described a situation involving performance and learning:

> The American parent's emphasis on the profitability of the JV clouded their judgement. They just could not see past the startup period. The losses distorted the attitudes of the American parent. Learning was never allowed to surface. Their attitude became, they [the Japanese partner] don't know anything so how can we learn from these people?

Chapter 2 indicated that the American parents often had a preoccupation with short-term financial performance. In the poor performing ventures, American firms seemed fixated on improving their return on investment, which meant first that resources which might have been committed to staff development or other learning efforts were directed toward improving JV performance, and second that American firm interest in the JVs declined.

Because the American partners were heavily focused on financial performance issues, learning often became a secondary and less tangible concern. While North Americans focused on the bottom line, the Japanese focused on improving productivity, quality, and delivery. For American managers, it was difficult to conceive that learning could be occurring in the face of poor performance. Consequently, there was a reluctance to commit to or even try out proposals generated at the JV level. This finding is consistent with Levinthal and March's (1993) argument that organizational learning oversamples successes and under-samples failures. As a result, learning processes tend to eliminate failures and sustained experimentation becomes difficult.

The relationship between learning and JV performance posed a paradoxical challenge for JV general managers. On the one hand, general managers were charged with generating an adequate financial return for the American parents; on the other hand, they were expected to act as the conduit for the parent's learning initiative. A focus on one objective detracted from the other. More importantly, when either learning or performance were less than satisfactory, there were implications for the assessment of the other objective. Thus, while poor performance can act as a barrier to learning, unexploited learning opportunities may lead to perceptions of unsatisfactory JV performance.

CONCLUSION

The framework of organizational learning presented at the outset of this chapter, in conjunction with data from the JV study, raises several important issues. Since organizations learn through their individual members, the individual aspects of organizational learning, involving both cognitive and behavioural change, cannot be ignored. As stated previously, individuals learn by identifying gaps or conflicts between their experience and their beliefs, and by resolving identified discrepancies through changes in their beliefs and behaviours. It was suggested that changes in beliefs occur more readily in the face of gaps than in the face of conflicts. We observed that managers expected to find gaps in their knowledge but instead found subtle discrepancies that were not easily interpreted. Since the JV experience conflicted with established belief systems, discrepancies were not always seen.

The first ingredient of individual learning, the noticing of discrepancies, is more likely to arise when an individual has a complex belief system. Therefore, experts with more complex belief systems should notice more discrepancies than novices with less complex belief systems. Resolution, the second ingredient, is more likely to occur in individuals where the belief systems have some flexibility. We found that firms with a deteriorating competitive position often had managers with the most entrenched belief systems. The fact that these firms had competitive problems may be traced to an unwillingness to cast off or unlearn past practices.

We also argue that even if a firm is open and accessible with its skills, individual managers must have the motivation and ability to notice the discrepancies. Thus, a key factor in a firm's ability to absorb new skills (i.e. its absorptiveness, using the concept suggested by Cohen and Levinthal (1990), is a sufficiently complex managerial belief system with which to notice and appreciate firm differences.

Hamel (1991) defined receptivity as the learning firm's ability to absorb skills from its partner. Receptivity can be analysed at three levels: individual, group, and organization. At the individual level, receptivity is closely linked with individual interpretation and, therefore, transparency and receptivity overlap as learning determinants. Without the ability to interpret what is happening in the JV environment, the individual becomes an empty conduit of information for other members in the organization. An inability to absorb new information may be confused with low transparency. Managers may blame their lack of learning, and failure to notice differences, on their partner's unwillingness to share information. In fact, the problem may be that individuals are unable to perceive differences because the partner knowledge is context-bound. Therefore, as a prerequisite to learning through JVs, managers must overcome the uncertainty and ambiguity surrounding their assessment of partner capabilities.

While receptivity may exist at the individual level, its absence at the organization level may indicate that senior managers are not receptive to the JV stimuli, perhaps because they are not directly involved in JV management. Thus, even if a group of individuals are able to share their learning through an integration process, without senior management receptivity, organizational learning will not occur.

Perhaps the most salient observation is the dynamic nature of learning and its determinants. Concepts such as intent, transparency, and receptivity should not be viewed as static. For a variety of reasons they may change over time. In several cases where the American firm did not have an initial learning intent, skill discrepancies became obvious and unavoidable. For example, an American firm that had prided itself on its high quality product status found its quality lacking when it attempted to supply a Japanese transplant automaker:

The American partner was considered a high quality domestic supplier and had a Q1 [highest quality] rating from Ford. However, in the JV we quickly discovered that to deal with the Japanese you have to be world class; we were only American class. We initially had problems meeting our Japanese customers' quality standards.

Most of the American firms in this study formed their JVs with an objective of learning from their Japanese partners, their expectations often were to learn 'what' the Japanese knew, rather than 'how' and 'why' the Japanese firms knew what they knew. Again, this raises the notion of knowledge as information (the 'what') and know-how (the 'how' and 'why'). Expectations about learning experiences typically revolved around clearly identifiable and visible activities. However, as General Motors discovered in its NUMMI venture, the most valuable learning experience was not associated with specific techniques but with an overall philosophy of organizing and competing. According to a JV vice president:

The American firm was somewhat naive in their learning expectations; they knew little about the overall Japanese way of doing things. Learning could occur only if there was a complete acceptance of the philosophy since all its parts were interconnected.

Chapter 8

Case vignettes

VIGNETTE 1 – JV FORMATION

For thirty years, Alpha Ltd (Alpha) had maintained a sales office in Japan. The office was established by a non-automotive division that had since been sold. Alpha kept the sales office open primarily to maintain contact with the Japanese market. In the mid-1980s, Alpha became interested in developing business with the growing transplant market in North America. Alpha's objective was to be a major player in the world's largest markets, but at that point lacked a significant Japanese presence.

Alpha considered forming a JV and used its sales office in Japan to review the industry for potential partners. Three companies were identified as potential JV partners. Alpha was considering its next step when Toyota's North American purchasing department asked Alpha to quote on a product for its new Georgetown, Kentucky plant. Alpha's vice president of manufacturing remarked, 'At that point we were still naive enough to believe that we might be able to get some transplant business without a Japanese connection.'

After the quotation was submitted, Toyota contacted Alpha about forming a JV to supply its new plant. Toyota was informed that Alpha was interested; this led to a trip to Japan arranged with Toyota's assistance. Several senior Alpha executives met with two potential JV partners, the number one and two suppliers for Toyota in Japan. The meetings were very formal and according to Alpha's vice president, 'We only saw their conference room.'

The next step was to have the potential Japanese partners come to North America. Both companies visited in May 1986, and 'we only showed them our conference room'. Neither Japanese company was interested in a wholly-owned North American investment because of unfamiliarity with the North American business environment.

Alpha management concluded that there was a better 'chemistry' with the larger supplier, Hito Inc. (Hito). Hito was one of the largest automotive suppliers in Japan and a long-standing member of Toyota's supplier association. They also thought that Toyota was very supportive of Alpha as a JV supplier and would like to see an Alpha–Hito JV. Alpha's vice president commented, 'I am not really sure of the extent to which Toyota influenced the JV formation but I think that Toyota and Hito worked together to make it happen.'

An initial problem in the formation process was that Hito wanted majority ownership. Alpha's vice president suspected that Hito sought majority ownership because that was what Toyota wanted. They also may have wanted to protect their technology. Alpha management knew they could not get majority ownership but held out and were successful in negotiating a 50–50 JV. After ten years, the JV agreement will be reviewed.

The JV was formed in December 1986, about one year after the first meetings in Japan. The vice president of manufacturing acknowledged that although Hito probably would like to see the JV develop some Big 3 work, 'it probably would never happen'. The VP was adamant that the JV would not be allowed to compete against Kappa. He commented, 'I know the implications of having a JV competing against its parents and I do not want to see it happen here.' The JV agreement specified that the venture would not be allowed to compete directly against the American parent. The JV was, however, allowed to introduce new products into the North American market for both domestic and transplant customers.

Initially, Hito was concerned that an American partner would not have the necessary patience for a long-term relationship. Hito thought that areas such as training would be sacrificed to get quick profitability. The VP assured them that 'we know the JV is different and we will look at the JV differently'. The VP assigned top Kappa managers to the JV and made his commitment to the venture known to Hito management.

Initial pro-forma financial statements were prepared with the expectation that there would be at least three years of losses. The original total investment by both partners was $14 million. The JV began operations in early 1988 and was profitable within eighteen months. The startup was one of Alpha's best and according to the VP, 'Hito was amazed by the speed of the startup and its quick profitability.' A major expansion took place in 1990 and JV sales of more than $100 million were anticipated within a few years.

For Alpha, the JV was an important learning experience. The primary learning focus was in the area of production. Alpha made an effort to give all its senior manufacturing personnel access to the JV and to send them to Japan to observe Japanese management firsthand. The second learning area involved marketing to Japanese companies. Since the JV was formed, Alpha was able to develop new business with two transplants. Without the knowledge gained from the JV, the new business could not have been developed.

VIGNETTE 2 – JV LEARNING POTENTIAL

Beta Corp. (Beta) was a large automotive supplier manufacturing components for the domestic Big 3. With its traditional market losing share, Beta saw a Japanese JV opportunity as a way to stem the losses expected from its domestic business. In 1987, Beta began discussions with Kinuko Manufacturing Inc. (Kinuko), a Japanese company closely linked with one of the largest Japanese car manufacturers. A JV agreement was reached that gave 60 per cent ownership to Beta. Kinuko was to be responsible for day-to-day operations. The JV would be primarily a tier-two supplier, selling to the wholly-owned subsidiary of the Japanese firm that owned 40 per cent of Kinuko.

Beta was motivated by two factors in forming the JV. First, Beta sought access to the expanding transplant market. Since its domestic automobile business was declining, the JV would help Beta to protect its market share. The JV was an extension of Beta's existing business and was expected to produce a product very similar to existing product lines. Second, Beta management saw the JV as an excellent opportunity to learn about Japanese management.

Like many other American automotive suppliers, Beta saw its customers losing market share to Japanese companies. In the early 1980s, Beta sent several groups of managers to Japan to 'find out what was really happening'. The managers visited various facilities in the same business as Beta. The result of those trips was the realization that technologically the Japanese plants were not radically different. The visitors saw equipment that was largely the same, although the plants were much better organized and more efficient.

Beta concluded that purchasing Japanese technology was not the answer. The Japanese were using more expensive raw materials and had the same equipment. In Beta's view, the differences had to be managerial. Beta had some idea of things like JIT and other techniques but senior management could not agree on what the real important differences were. They decided that a JV would help them learn from the Japanese. As a Beta manager commented, 'Our feeling was that we might not get rich from the JV but at least we could learn a lot about Japanese management.'

VIGNETTE 3 – JV FAILURE

In 1984, the Japanese firm, Noro Inc. (Noro) was encouraged by its primary Japanese customer to establish a plant in North America. Noro had some experience with JVs and decided that a JV would be the best strategy for a North American investment. Noro management made several trips to North America in search of a suitable partner.

Meanwhile, Sigma Systems Ltd. (Sigma), an automotive supplier based in Detroit, had been scouting around Japan for potential JV partners and sales contracts. Sigma was currently involved in a small, low-tech job for Noro's main Japanese customer's North American division. Noro, aware that the Japanese customer was satisfied with its relationship with Sigma, contacted Sigma about the possibility of forming a JV. A JV agreement with Sigma holding a 60 per cent interest was signed and the JV began operations in 1985. The JV was established initially to supply a single transplant, Noro's main Japanese customer. The partners agreed that Noro would supply all the technical resources and Sigma would take care of the management.

After two years of operations, Sigma became very concerned that the JV was still losing money. According to the JV general manager, 'Sigma wanted to make a quick buck; they were sceptical of making long-term investments. They saw the JV as a way to make some money and expected a profit in two years.' Noro, however, had a very different perspective. 'Noro expected the JV to lose money for about five or six years. Unfortunately, they never communicated this to Sigma and no explicit business plan was prepared.'

Despite continuing to lose money, the JV was increasing its market share and attracted several new customers, including Ford and General Motors. When an expansion became necessary, Sigma declined to contribute any new capital. Thus, Noro financed the expansion and increased its JV interest from 40 per cent to 45 per cent. After a second expansion a short time later, Noro's interest increased to 49 per cent. Sigma, in the meantime,

was going berserk because the JV was losing much more money than was anticipated. They were also concerned that Noro did not seem nearly as upset about the financial situation as they were. Sigma did not really understand Noro's expectations about the business.

In 1990, it became obvious that a major expansion would be necessary. Over the past four years, sales had increased from $7 million to more than $40 million. Plans were put in place to add another building that would double the size of the company from 300 to 600 employees. Sigma, however, was gradually withdrawing from the JV. With the latest expansion, Sigma's JV interest decreased to 30 per cent and the general manager anticipated that soon the JV would be terminated. The general manager described Sigma's attitude toward the JV:

> Sigma is in a different business than Noro. Because Sigma is in a different business than Noro, it's hard for them to understand the JV business. . . . They [Sigma] got in over their heads financially. Even if they knew what they had to do to change, they could not afford to do it.

VIGNETTE 4 – PERFORMANCE AND LEARNING

JV discussions between Theta Ltd (Theta), based in Cleveland, and Tokyo-based Miyuki Corp. (Miyuki) started in 1987. A JV was formed a year later and began operations in 1988. Neither partner was a clear initiator of the venture; both firms were interested in forming a JV to serve the North American transplant market.

The JV was regarded as an important strategic opportunity by Theta senior management, both from market share and learning perspectives. The JV executive vice president (EVP) commented, 'Theta, and especially the Chairman, saw the JV as a shining star and the wave of the future for Theta.'

For Miyuki, the JV helped resolve some uncertainty about a US operation. Miyuki had never operated outside Japan and had little international market experience. The EVP also thought that Miyuki was encouraged by their largest Japanese customer to form a JV, since this firm was anxious to increase domestic content in its North American-produced cars. Although Miyuki could have established a wholly-owned North American subsidiary and still contributed to the transplant's domestic content, a JV with an American firm created domestic content that did not originate entirely with a Japanese company.

The JV agreement gave majority ownership to Theta (60 per cent) and operating management control to Miyuki. Unfortunately, the first management team had to be replaced after a short period because it was obvious to both partners that serious problems had developed. The Japanese and American managers had largely stopped talking to each other and were making few joint decisions. Large financial losses and operating inefficiencies compounded the problem. The EVP (not part of the initial management team) explained:

> The initial management teams were second rate. Theta selected a retired Theta plant manager as its senior JV representative and Miyuki did not send any good people. Both partners decided that the second time they had to put in top people. The new management team improved communication between the partners and gave Theta access to more information than with the old team. Unfortunately, the new information was mostly bad news.

The JV's financial situation became a major cause of concern to Theta management. When the JV started losing money and missing its business plans, 'panic set in at Theta'. Theta management began to question Miyuki about why the losses were occurring and how long before the JV would become profitable. Theta wanted to see a plan in place that would take the JV to profitability or at least breakeven. The EVP explained:

> The discussions with Miyuki frustrated Theta because they believed that Miyuki was withholding information from them. Miyuki was unable to be specific about when the JV would become profitable. Miyuki was focused on different aspects of the business. Theta wanted to know about profit; Miyuki was more concerned with making the operation more efficient and satisfying their customer's needs.
>
> Unfortunately, during the JV discussions, no specific profit margins were known or established prior to the formation of the JV. Consequently, what Theta thought they were going in with and the reality were two different things. Theta's initial expectations about profit were not even close to being met.
>
> Theta management felt that they were being forced to ask questions because of all the problems. Miyuki would not or could not provide any answers. And Miyuki regarded the questions as a breach of trust and inappropriate in a working relationship based on trust. The two partners became alienated from each other. Theta began to think that everyone in the JV was nuts. They also began to question Miyuki's credibility and thought, 'Are they [Miyuki] doing this to force us out of the JV?'

The EVP provided a perspective on why the two partners failed to agree on the JV objectives.

The Japanese look at everything from a longer-term perspective. They saw that the JV would go through various stages, with profitability being several years away. The Americans wanted the profitability stage to occur much faster. This attitude upset the Japanese order because their view is if you can satisfy the customer and get costs under control, you will eventually make a profit. But that profit probably would not be at the level expected by an American company.

Theta started doubting both its original motives for being in the JV and the capabilities of its Japanese partner. Meanwhile, financial performance showed no signs of improving. Despite forming the JV with an explicit learning objective, the JV's large losses led Theta to believe that there was no expertise to be learned.

The EVP was convinced that even if the JV was in a breakeven position, Theta would have said, 'Let's hope for the future.' However, that did not seem likely in the foreseeable future so Theta decided to end the JV. They offered their share of the venture to Miyuki. Miyuki was somewhat surprised that Theta wanted to end the relationship since the JV had been in operation less than three years. However, Theta management had had enough and wanted out.

Miyuki agreed to purchase its JV partner's interest and operate the JV as a wholly-owned company. Subsequent to the JV termination, Miyuki went to its two largest Japanese customers and negotiated large price increases, which were, according to the EVP, 'much larger than you could ever get with a Big 3 company'. Miyuki also brought over twelve engineers from Japan to help sort out operational problems. The EVP agreed to remain with the company for a year to manage the transition from JV to full ownership. From the EVP's perspective, 'Miyuki will not let this company fail. It will be a good transplant supplier, help the transplants get local content, but never make much money.'

VIGNETTE 5 – HIGH LEARNING POTENTIAL, LOW OUTCOME

In the mid-1980s, Enzo Inc. (Enzo), a Japanese automotive parts producer, was under pressure to supply its primary customer from an American plant. However, Enzo was reluctant to establish a wholly-owned facility in the United States. At the same time, a management team from an American firm, Anson Corp. (Anson), was looking for a Japanese partner. In March 1988, Enzo and Anson signed a technical assistance agreement. Enzo would bring several engineers to the United States and teach Anson how to manufacture to the Japanese customer's specifications. Anson would be the transplant supplier and Enzo would provide the technical assistance to get them going.

Very quickly the partners realized that the technical assistance agreement would not work. According to the JV president:

> There was no way Anson could meet the transplant's needs. When the transplant says jump, you jump. Anson had never done business that way. If there is a problem with the transplant you have to react in an hour. In Anson's experience, if there are problems they may get around to them in a week or two.

Other than prototypes and samples, Anson never manufactured any products for the transplant customer. In June 1989, the partners decided they needed to develop a more integrated relationship and formed a 50–50 JV. The JV was established in vacant space in an existing Anson plant to give the JV access to Anson's specialized equipment and minimize the initial investment. The main equipment for the plant came from Japan. At the transplant's insistence, the plant was set up as closely as possible to be a replica of a Japanese plant.

By 1991 the JV was in serious financial difficulty, at which point the Anson board decided that no further capital would be invested in the JV. By 1992 the JV had improved its financial position and in August 1992 broke even for the first time. After several more small losses, the JV again approached breakeven in January 1993 and became profitable in subsequent periods. According to both JV and parent managers, the JV was achieving greater productivity and lower defect rates than Anson.

For several reasons, this JV created a high learning potential for the American parent.

1 The JV was located in an existing American parent less than a mile from the Anson corporate offices and, therefore, Anson managers could easily visit and interact with JV managers.
2 The Japanese parent was explicit in indicating a willingness to share its technology with Anson.
3 The JV products were functionally similar to Anson products, which meant that the Anson managers were familiar with the technology used in the JV.
4 The JV was achieving greater productivity and lower defect rates than Anson.
5 By its fourth year of operation the JV had become one of its primary transplant customer's most reliable suppliers, indicating that the JV was producing very high-quality products.

6 Anson worked closely with the JV as an intermediate processor, allowing for interaction between parent and JV manufacturing personnel.

Anson management indicated that one of their primary JV objectives was to learn from the JV. Despite this initial learning intent and the high learning potential, over three years of observation, little in the way of learning systems were implemented and according to senior Anson managers, the learning experience was less than satisfactory. Anson's president commented:

> The two sides are too different. They are like oil and water. The JV is in a different business. They do not have traditional customer relationships and they make a handful of parts compared to us. Everything takes so long to get done there. They are experts at nitpicking.

Anson treated the JV like an autonomous subsidiary rather than a closely related division. There were few interactions between the JV and Anson at the managerial level and top management at Anson seemed unwilling to initiate learning efforts. For example, Enzo offered to share some proprietary process technology with its American partner at no cost. The technology was used in the JV and was therefore very visible to American partner managers. The offer was communicated in a written memo from a JV manager to the American partner president. The American firm never followed up on the offer.

VIGNETTE 6 – LOW LEARNING POTENTIAL, HIGH OUTCOME

In 1987, Hiruki Inc. (Hiruki), a large Japanese trading company, began looking for a partner in the United States to supply the transplants. Hiruki wanted a local partner because of the language differences and because an American firm would be familiar with local purchasing practices. Also, Hiruki operated primarily as a trading company in the United States and was not directly involved in manufacturing.

When IRL Technology Inc. (IRL), the American partner, was approached by Hiruki, it was seen as an excellent business opportunity for several reasons:

1 It would be a 'feather in IRL's cap' to become involved with Hiruki and be perceived as having a relationship with the transplants.
2 It would give IRL a feel for worldwide operations in their industry.
3 It could lead to future opportunities with Hiruki.

Both companies recognized the need to form a JV and were supportive of the other. The original objective was for the JV to produce primarily for the transplant markets (mainly automotive suppliers) and to work in a JIT environment. When negotiations to form the JV were started, IRL management made it clear that they were only willing to be involved if they managed the JV. According to the first JV president, 'We have a quality reputation which we should be able to carry over to the JV.' His position was that IRL had the skills in manufacturing; Hiruki was not bringing manufacturing skills to the table (at least not directly; in Japan Hiruki is involved in manufacturing operations).

The JV was set up with a management agreement with IRL. IRL provided accounting, purchasing, technical service, sales support for domestic sales, and information processing support for the JV. This meant that IRL managers had no choice but be involved in the JV. In many respects, IRL employees did not differentiate the two JV plants from IRL plants because the two used the same systems. The JV paid IRL a management fee for this service.

The JV president worked out of the IRL head office and was closely associated with IRL. IRL assigned a plant manager to each of the JV plants and Hiruki assigned a sales manager. Although IRL was supposed to have manufacturing control, Hiruki was involved, as the JV president explained:

Even though their role is supposed to be confined to sales, the Japanese managers know every inch of the plant and try to influence the plant management.

This JV was classified as creating low learning potential for several reasons:

1 The division of responsibility did not give IRL complete exposure to the JV operations. IRL controlled operations management (plant managers), the manufacturing process equipment, and administrative functions. The plant was built using IRL construction personnel. Hiruki's role was limited to sales – the JV agreement explicitly stated that Hiruki would supply the customer orders.
2 IRL did not have a strong learning intent.
3 Because Hiruki was a large trading company, there was not a specific partner operation that could be directly studied. The partner was involved in many different trading and service activities.

Despite the low learning potential, IRL management described the JV as a very positive learning experience. In terms of JV product quality, the JV president said that although he hated to admit it, the quality of the JV product was superior to that in the parent. 'The JV has become more meticulous because the customers demand it.' The JV has helped IRL to understand the importance of forward planning and customer service in a very competitive environment.

Several factors contributed to the strong learning outcome:

1 The JV was profitable after only a few months, which meant that financial issues did not obscure the learning experience.

2 The JV was very closely integrated with IRL, both operationally and strategically.

3 IRL was an industry leader and was not a 'laggard' in comparison with Hiruki. That may have helped in the learning process because as an industry leader, the amount of unlearning is less than in the case of the laggard.

4 The main 'lesson' for IRL was the notion of forward vision and planning for the future. In this venture the technology was controlled by IRL, limiting the opportunities for the transfer of technology. Therefore, the learning experience had to be 'idea' oriented: long-term business plans, customer support, no wastage, etc. These are philosophical and very managerial in nature.

The Japanese VP in the JV described IRL managers as good students. 'They are positively absorbing things from their JV experience, particularly the need for long-term investment.' However, he made an interesting comment: 'They never ask direct questions.'

VIGNETTE 7 – KNOWLEDGE MANAGEMENT

Iota Ltd. (Iota) and Yakyu Inc. (Yakyu) had a relationship going back twenty-five years. The firms had various licensing agreements and an agreement not to compete against each other. Iota concentrated on its North American home market plus most of Europe while Yakyu focused on Japan and other Asian countries.

The president of Iota initiated the JV. He was close to Yakyu management and knew the firm wanted a North American operation. He also knew that Yakyu's primary Japanese customer wanted Yakyu to invest in North America. Prior to forming the JV, the Japanese auto-maker shipped parts from Japan. However, because of the shipping costs and the Japanese customer's objective of increasing domestic content, the Japanese customer sought North American suppliers. The Japanese automaker did not believe it could get satisfactory quality from a North

American supplier and, therefore, wanted to deal with Yakyu or another Japanese supplier. Because Yakyu and Iota had a non-competing agreement, Yakyu had little choice but to form a JV with Iota or lose the market to their Japanese competitors who had already formed a US JV.

The JV, a 50–50 agreement, began operating in 1986 in a new plant. The president of Iota was designated as the JV president. The JV president selected an Iota manager to be the executive vice president (EVP) of the JV and the senior operating manager in the venture. According to the EVP:

> The presidency effectively gives Iota managerial control. But Yakyu tries to influence me in the way I manage the JV. Our main customer is Yakyu's main customer in Japan so Yakyu wants to make sure that the JV does not screw up.

The EVP went on to describe the management style in the JV.

> This is not a Japanese company. It is an American company that has adopted aspects of Japanese and American management. Originally, our objective was to run the plant like a Japanese company. There would be uniforms, an open office concept, etc. That did not last long. The first team of Japanese was replaced entirely. The open office concept did not work because there was not enough space and it was too disconcerting because there was no privacy.

The JV began operations strictly as a transplant supplier, but after three years developed some business with two domestic automakers. The JV had large losses in its first four years of operation. From Iota's perspective, the major factor contributing to the losses was pricing with the primary transplant customer. The American firm considered the price structure unreasonable and pressed Yakyu to make some changes. The EVP explained:

> It took us about one year to convince the Japanese that they had to renegotiate prices with the customer. It involved some real battles but we knew we were doing a good job. Finally, we went to the transplant and said enough is enough. We were able to settle on new price levels with genuine margins that are comfortable for us. We have taken over estimation from Yakyu and are now doing it in the JV. The bleeding has been stopped and soon the JV will be profitable. Iota is now satisfied with the JV performance and is willing to put some more money into the JV. Yakyu was never really concerned and was always willing to contribute additional capital. With them everything was always okay.

The EVP was convinced that the JV represented an excellent learning opportunity for Iota. He identified some key learning areas:

1 The importance of a complete customer orientation at all levels of the organization. Our Japanese customers have created that philosophy in the JV. As a result, the JV product is far superior to anything that Iota can produce.

2 The improvement in quality that is possible when the customer demands continual improvement and is willing to help the supplier achieve it. Iota talks about quality, but in the JV we do it.

3 Simple things like training the workforce before they operate machines and the importance of maintenance and cleanliness in the plant.

4 How to run a JIT plant. This is the only true JIT plant that Iota has. We make four shipments a day to our major Japanese customer. They talk about a four-hour window for shipment.

5 Information distribution in the JV. Everybody right down to the bottom of the organization gets more information [than in Iota]. They are given information on business plans, profit and loss, and other areas. People may not understand it but they appreciate that they are being given the opportunity to get involved.

Initially, Iota management seemed reluctant to learn from the JV. The EVP indicated that parent managers were given an open invitation to visit and tour the JV operation. While there was some response, 'There was apparently some resentment against Japanese companies in Iota.'

However, as the JV performance improved and the domestic automotive industry experienced a downturn, Iota management began to express a greater interest in JV activities. The JV management wanted to expand the JV plant and were being supported by Iota. Iota, apparently willing to become more involved in the JV operation, asked the EVP to prepare some expansion plans. The EVP commented:

With the downturn in the auto industry, the JV is now starting to beat the other Iota plants. They are losing money and the JV is clearly superior in terms of quality and efficiency. Iota can no longer ignore the differences between the JV and the Iota plants.

Iota managers began to visit the JV and were slowly changing their minds about it. The plant manager for the largest Iota plant recently visited the JV. According to the EVP, 'There is still some work to be done in terms of upper management's perception of the JV. But, the relationship between the JV and Iota is now a genuine partnership.'

Iota was actively involved in exploiting the learning potential of its JV. Various mechanisms were used to gain access to alliance knowledge. These included:

1 Iota management have studied various aspects of the JV's operation, including its use of employee involvement programmes, *kaizen* teams, and its scheduling system. Iota has also studied some of the JV's process innovations, one of which the JV considers proprietary.

2 Several JV managers were promoted to positions within Iota. One manager was promoted into an Iota staff training position at Iota HQ. Several engineers have also been promoted.

3 Iota senior management are committed to the JV and to an Asian connection. The JV is the strongest Asian connection. The president of Iota has a very close relationship with the former Japanese parent chairman.

4 Iota has formed 'teams' to share information on forming and fabrication. The idea is that representatives from the various Iota plants (the JV included) will get together regularly and share information.

5 Iota has set up what it calls 'gatekeepers', which are units of the company responsible for certain aspects of manufacturing. The gatekeeper is expected to be available to all units of the company interested in the specific process or technology. The JV was asked to be the gatekeeper for JIT.

6 Iota has several engineers temporarily working in Japan in the Japanese parent organization.

7 Iota and the Japanese parent have initiated a joint engineering project. A piece of manufacturing equipment will be made by the Japanese partner in Japan, with an American engineer visiting Japan during the project period. The equipment will be installed in an Iota plant and Iota will pay Yakyu for the developmental work.

8 More than 15 employees in the JV have visited Japan.

Chapter 9

Learning and JV stability

This chapter was co-authored by
Paul W. Beamish

This chapter examines the relationship between learning, collaborative knowledge and IJV stability. If IJVs are inherently unstable organizational forms, as researchers and managers have suggested, why do some ventures survive and prosper for many years? This chapter argues that foreign partner knowledge of the local economic, political, and cultural environments is a critical factor in the stability of IJVs. When the foreign partner is no longer satisfied with access to local knowledge and seeks to acquire this knowledge, the probability of JV instability increases substantially. This chapter suggests that if managers are aware of the factors influencing JV stability, they may be able to prevent or control for premature changes in partner relationships.

IJVs AND INSTABILITY

Despite the surge in the popularity of international alliances, alliances are often described as inherently unstable organizational forms. Porter (1990), for example, observed that alliances involve significant costs in terms of coordination, reconciling goals with an independent entity, and creating competitors. Porter suggested that these costs make many alliances transitional rather than stable arrangements and, therefore, alliances are rarely a sustainable means for creating competitive advantage. Supporting that argument, several empirical studies of alliances have found instability rates of close to 50 per cent (Beamish 1985; Bleeke and Ernst 1991).

Alliances and JVs have also been described as a 'race to learn', with the partner learning the fastest dominating the relationship (Hamel *et al.* 1989). In this scenario of inevitable instability there are clear winners and losers. Yet some international alliances survive and prosper for many years, with both sides becoming more competitive in a win–win relationship. Thus, the issue central to this chapter is why some JVs are more stable than others.

Unlike alliances such as R&D partnerships or licensing agreements, equity JVs create new organizational entities distinct from their parents. JVs also differ from other alliances in terms of formation objectives and, therefore, statements generalizing about the instability of alliances should be interpreted carefully. The factors associated with JV instability are not necessarily the same as those for other types of alliances. For example, licensing agreements and technology sharing arrangements have gained notoriety as vehicles for licensee firms to build their own skill base and shift the alliance balance of power in their favor. Reich and Mankin (1986) consider the competitive implications of sharing technology with a potential competitor. They focus on high-technology agreements in which the US partner acquired and distributed Japanese products; in effect, outsourcing relationships. Note that these are not JVs according to our definition.

In addition to the JV data used in the previous chapters, two additional sources of data are introduced:

1 An indepth study of Toppan Moore,[1] a large, Japan-based JV between Toppan Printing and Moore Corporation.
2 Case studies of five developing country JVs in the Caribbean.[2]

While all the JVs involved a variety of strategic objectives, they were similar in involving a foreign partner seeking a viable operational stake in its local partner's home country. Market access as an important objective of the foreign partner is discussed by Killing (1983), Kogut (1988), and Root (1988).

To establish an operational presence in a country requires access to local knowledge as a means of overcoming market uncertainties (Stopford and Wells 1972). When a foreign firm does not have that knowledge, a JV may be used to gain access quickly to a local partner's knowledge base. We propose that as the foreign partner's local knowledge and commitment to acquire local knowledge increases, the probability of JV instability also increases. This argument complements the well-developed theme in the international management literature concerning the frequent conflict between global and local optimization of strategy (e.g. Bartlett and Ghoshal 1989; Franko 1971). Given these conflicting demands, what happens when a multinational enterprise (MNE) involved in an IJV decides to pursue a localization strategy? We will argue that the MNE's acquisition of local knowledge enables the MNE to make the transition from JV to subsidiary. We will also suggest that an important distinction has to be made between the local knowledge effect on stability, and the decision to acquire the knowledge. For example, an MNE may decide that its JV should be a wholly-owned subsidiary. Unless the MNE has acquired the local knowledge necessary to manage the venture autonomously, a wholly-owned subsidiary is not a viable option.

Thus, the acquisition of local knowledge can facilitate the transition to subsidiary and is a necessary factor in the decision. For example, the American firm, Ralston Purina, ended its twenty-year venture with Taiyo Fishery Company and established a wholly-owned subsidiary in Japan. Having gained experience and local knowledge in Japan, Ralston Purina management apparently decided that a Japanese partner was no longer necessary.

Even if local knowledge is acquired, an MNE may decide that a JV is preferred to a subsidiary. A JV can provide various economic, political, and market access benefits to foreign partners, benefits which would be lost if the JV were terminated. Therefore, we do not propose that JVs will always become unstable when the foreign partner acquires local knowledge. Rather, we argue that the probability of instability increases when local knowledge is acquired, because an MNE's need for its local partner is reduced.

The chapter is organized as follows. In the first section, the concept of JV stability and its relationship with foreign partner knowledge is developed. The second section considers the value of local knowledge to the foreign partner and identifies factors that influence foreign partner acquisition of local knowledge. From the perspective that instability is controllable, the third section identifies several considerations for JV managers.

THE CONCEPT OF IJV INSTABILITY

JVs combine resources from more than one organization. Generally, the venture management tasks are shared or split between the partners and there is some symmetry in partner objectives. However, unlike licensing agreements or supplier relationships, contractual agreements between JV partners are often executed under conditions of high uncertainty and, therefore, it is unlikely that all future contingencies can be anticipated at the outset. As JVs grow they may develop an identity and culture distinct from that of the parents, adding to problems of coordination. These problems are compounded when the parents are from different countries.

What is JV instability?

Several definitions of instability have been used in the JV literature. One perspective considers both a shift in JV control and venture termination as evidence of instability (Killing 1983). Other researchers have adopted a narrower view, using venture termination as the sole indicator of instability (Kogut 1989). However, a JV cannot be considered unstable simply because its lifespan is short. All relationships between firms face new challenges that threaten to change or terminate the basis for cooperation. Sometimes terminations are planned and anticipated by the parties involved. Ventures may also be terminated as a matter of policy when there is a change in parent ownership or management. In our data there were several cases where a change in parent ownership precipitated termination because the new parent had a policy against JV involvement. The performance of the ventures prior to termination was satisfactory. These ventures would not be classified as unstable ventures. In other cases, difficulties associated with ending a relationship may create a rationale for maintaining an existing JV that would otherwise be terminated.

We maintain that instability should be linked with unplanned equity changes or major reorganizations. Usually, instability will result in premature JV termination, either when one partner acquires the JV business or the venture is dissolved. A complicating factor is that JV termination will not always be a mutual decision (Parkhe 1991). Premature termination may be precipitated by the actions of one partner. For example, we observed several cases where the Japanese partner was clearly trying to learn from its American partner in order to erase dependency on the partner. The 'learning' partners and 'teaching' partners had very different longevity objectives. These ventures would be classified as unstable because termination was premature from the perspective of the teaching partner. Thus, if at least one of the partners anticipates a long-term relationship, premature termination of the venture would constitute instability.

In most IJVs the partners do not have a specific plan for the termination of their ventures.[3] In the Japanese–American sample, none of the American partners planned on early termination. These firms expected their JVs to become long-term relationships. However, the ventures often became unstable when, after venture formation, partner objectives diverged. On that basis, JV instability is defined as a major change in relationship status that was unplanned from one or both partners' perspectives.

However, it is important to emphasize that we do not equate the longevity of a JV with JV success. Many firms view JVs as intentionally temporary and recognize that their ventures will not last indefinitely. If a JV termination is an orderly and mutually planned event, the JV may well be evaluated as extremely successful. In fact, a JV that is prematurely terminated may also be evaluated as successful, depending on the criteria used to evaluate performance. For example, in several unstable Japanese–American JVs in this study, the American partners faced with premature termination were willing to concede that their venture experience was valuable in providing exposure to transplant customers. In sum, JV performance is a very complex area. We see instability as only one of various factors in the performance equation.

Local knowledge and the foreign partner

Various factors have been identified as causes of JV instability, including changes in partners' strategic missions, changes in importance of the JV to the parents, changes in the partners' relative bargaining power, and an increase in the competitive rivalry between partners (Harrigan and Newman 1990). While the existence of these factors provides a strong indication that venture termination or reorganization may be imminent, our research suggests that these factors are symptoms of instability rather than its root cause. In the case of IJVs there is a more powerful explanatory factor for instability: the extent of local knowledge acquisition by the foreign partner.

As indicated, our primary interest is JVs in which the foreign partner seeks to expand its geographic scope of operations. If a JV is used, it would be unusual for the local partner not to contribute some local knowledge. When government legislation prohibits wholly-owned subsidiaries, silent partners contributing little more than a means to bypass legislation may be used. However, with the liberalizing of trade and investment, particularly in developing countries, fewer countries continue to mandate the use of JVs for foreign investment.

Even if technology sourcing or sharing risk are important objectives, if the venture is international, it is likely that the local partner is able and expected to possess knowledge of the local market, politics, and/or culture. In the Caribbean case studies, the five MNE partners used their JVs to introduce existing products into new markets. The primary JV motive in each case was access to specific local knowledge possessed by the local JV partners (there was no government requirement to use the JV form).

Nine years after the original data collection, JV general managers were asked the question 'Does the foreign partner have a long-term need for the local partner?' In all cases the answer was yes. Despite many years of accumulated experience in the local market, the foreign partners continued to depend on their local partners for specialized local knowledge. The foreign partners lack of local knowledge necessary to operate autonomously in the local market was a key factor in the continued venture stability.

Instability as a function of the foreign partner's knowledge

A direct relationship is proposed between instability and the foreign partner's knowledge of local market, political, and cultural conditions. As the foreign partner increases its local country knowledge, instability in the JV relationship becomes more probable because of a shift in the foreign partner's bargaining power. This shift is accompanied by the dissipation of mutual partner need that existed at the time of JV formation. The acquisition of local knowledge enables the foreign partner to consider a wholly-owned subsidiary and eliminate the cooperative relationship.

As opposed to the foreign partner building a local knowledge base, the local partner may acquire the skills of its foreign partner, making the JV redundant. However, the 'skilling' of the local partner (or the de-skilling of the foreign partner) is a rarer event. First, as a JV is a separate entity, the local partner may have difficulty penetrating the venture boundaries to gain access to foreign partner skills. (Because there are fewer boundaries in a non-equity technology sharing relationship, there is a higher risk that organizational skills may be appropriated by a partner.) Second, even if local partners have unhindered access to partner skills, the learning required to eliminate a partner dependency is usually more difficult for the local partner than the foreign partner. The NUMMI JV between General Motors and Toyota illustrates this point. Badaracco (1991) described how Toyota was able to deploy its new local knowledge in a wholly-owned US plant in Georgetown, Kentucky.

A reduction in the foreign partner's JV commitment and partner need does not always mean that the foreign partner will acquire the JV business or establish a subsidiary. As the foreign partner increases its local knowledge various outcomes are possible, identified previously as symptoms of JV instability. For example, an increase in knowledge that erased the partner dependency, coupled with a desire to maintain a local market presence were the circumstances prompting Ralston Purina, Bayer AG, and Monsanto Co. to convert alliances to subsidiaries in

Japan (Ono 1991). Alternatively, as the foreign partner learns about local market realities, a decision may be made to withdraw from the market. Or, the foreign partner may seek a more prominent role in the management of the JV, leading to conflict over the division of control, which in turn could lead to an unstable relationship.

TOPPAN MOORE[4]

The Toppan Moore JV provides further support for our arguments. Although less prominent than JVs such as Fuji–Xerox and Yokogawa–Hewlett Packard, Toppan Moore became one of the largest and most successful Japan-based IJVs. With 1993 revenues of more than $1.5 billion and more than 3,000 employees, Toppan Moore was Japan's largest business forms company and third largest printing company. The firm was established in 1965 as a JV between Toppan Printing and Moore Corporation of Canada. Founded in 1900, Toppan Printing was the largest printing company in Asia and one of the world's largest printing companies with 1993 revenues of more than $10 billion. By 1993, the Toppan Group comprised over 100 companies, with 19 overseas subsidiaries employing 2,200 people in the United States, Asia, and Europe. Toronto-based Moore Corporation (Moore) was the world's largest manufacturer of business forms and a leader in new product development. In 1993, Moore sales were $2.3 billion.

The JV agreement specified that Toppan Printing, with 55 per cent of the equity, would have responsibility for the venture's operation and developing its business plan. Moore, with a 45 per cent share, would be responsible for supplying the production technology for making business forms. Initially, the venture would use Toppan Printing's salesforce and sell products to Toppan Printing's major customers. Sales and production planning would be independent of both parents, and cost and pricing principles would follow Moore's methods. The JV's initial management team was drawn almost exclusively from Toppan Printing. A vice president, appointed from Moore, remained in Toronto and had minimal substantive responsibility for managing the venture. The current vice president appointed from Moore explained:

> Moore accepted not having a bigger formal role in the JV because we didn't know a lot about the Japanese market in the beginning. We knew that for Toppan Printing, the JV was an outgrowth of what they were doing with an existing business forms business. We saw our role as bringing proven sales and production methods into the

venture, and we were willing to allow Toppan Moore to operate fairly autonomously. Because of the royalty arrangement, we were confident that the people in the JV would feel compelled to make it a success.

As the demand for business forms increased dramatically in the 1970s and 1980s, Toppan Moore experienced a rapid growth in sales. Subsidiaries were established to disperse headquarters functions and to increase responsiveness to local markets. Several JVs in Southeast Asia were formed and Toppan Moore became an important link in the global product/service networks of Toppan Printing and Moore Corporation.

Once a year, managers from Toppan Moore and Moore met for an open sharing of technical information. Although the JV had initially depended heavily on Moore's production technology, it had modified products to meet the requirements of Japanese customers, developed its own production know-how, and was bringing new products to market. The Japanese President of Toppan Moore described the evolution of Toppan Moore:

> So far, Toppan Moore has enjoyed immense success. This is not the norm for many JVs in Japan. One of the reasons is that Moore provided good circumstances for the development of the company. Moore made a sincere effort to launch the company. They gave us a lot of autonomy. They didn't interfere. We were able to adopt certain managerial methods and arrange them to fit with Japanese business customs. Moore looks at Toppan Moore as a young company, and they have a long-term view of its growth. For instance, Moore has never asked us to have a detailed strategic plan. We make decisions on personnel, investment, and fund raising without detailed consultation. We are able to manage freely, and we have adopted many Japanese principles, such as a long-term focus, interdependence among companies, business diversification, and a management style based on loyalty and human feeling. Toppan Moore is very much a traditional Japanese company.

Several insights can be drawn from the Toppan Moore case. Besides meeting government restrictions on foreign direct investment in Japan, Moore needed access to its Japanese partner's distribution channels. As the JV developed, that access became less critical because the JV developed its own channels. Moore continued with technological and marketing contributions but by playing a minimal role in Toppan Moore's operational management, allowed the venture to evolve into what the president called a 'a traditional Japanese company'. Even after twenty-seven years in the Japanese market it is questionable whether Moore could autonomously operate as effectively in Japan.

Considering that Moore, the leading firm in its industry worldwide, contributed the manufacturing and product technology and needed 'only' to learn how to market its products in Japan, why did the JV survive and why did Moore adopt a seemingly passive knowledge accumulation strategy? The answer may be that Moore, recognizing its limitations, continued to value the local knowledge contributions of its Japanese partner. For example, Toppan Printing continued to be a source of managers for the JV. In any event, Moore's decision not to expand aggressively its local Japanese knowledge base supports our stability proposition. As well, it is important to note that Moore's decision not to pursue aggressive localization efforts is in no way a reflection on its ability to do so. Moore's relationship with Toppan Printing suggests that Moore's competitive advantage is maximized by maintaining stability. General Electric has followed a similar strategy with its successful Japanese JVs. GE has leveraged its Japanese partners' names to recruit personnel for its JVs and allowed its JVs to develop into independent companies without interference from the parents in day-to-day management (Turpin 1993).

JAPANESE JVs IN NORTH AMERICA

We now return to the sample of Japanese–American JVs for further evidence of the relationship between stability and local knowledge. As discussed earlier, the predominant American partner objective in these JVs was access to Japanese transplant automakers in North America.

A test of the stability proposition

The Japanese–American JVs provided an opportunity to test the stability proposition by examining the cases of instability. At the time of data collection, there were eleven cases of instability, all terminations or major equity changes that were unplanned from the perspective of the American partner. Based on our arguments, the unstable ventures should have two main properties. One, rather than JV dissolution, the unstable JVs should become wholly-owned or majority-owned Japanese companies. None of the terminations in the sample involved dissolution of the JV business. Ten of the unstable JVs had become, or were in the process of becoming, wholly-owned subsidiaries of the Japanese partners. In the one case where the American partner acquired full ownership of a terminated JV, an American partner executive indicated that the Japanese firm had not abandoned the North American market and was planning to re-enter in another form.

Two, the unstable ventures should be predominantly engaged in supplying transplants rather than US automakers. The rationale is that if the foreign partners are familiar with the customer (the transplants), the local knowledge learning task is easier because it excludes customer knowledge. We found that nine of the eleven unstable ventures were exclusively transplant suppliers. Given the second property, we were able to test the knowledge–instability proposition.

The JV knowledge base at the time of venture formation, based on the partner contributions, should be a good predictor of instability because it provides evidence as to the amount of knowledge that the foreign partner needs to compete autonomously. Specifically, the ventures in which the Japanese partners controlled key knowledge inputs should be most prone to instability.

For the JVs to become operational, we assumed that three broad areas of knowledge were required within the venture: customer knowledge, manufacturing product and process knowledge, and local operational knowledge. (Other types of knowledge can be identified; we focused on these three because of the nature of the ventures.) Since the local partner had a monopoly on local operational knowledge, only the customer and manufacturing knowledge had the potential to be contributed by either partner.

Based on the detailed interview reports, there were three steps in the classification process for partner knowledge contributions. First, the ventures were classified on the basis of customer knowledge by determining which partner contributed the customer access: Japanese, American, or shared. Second, using the same three categories, the ventures were classified on the basis of which partner contributed the manufacturing technology used in the JV. These two classifications provided the basis for the final classification. If both customer and manufacturing knowledge were contributed by the Japanese partner, the venture was classified as a Japanese knowledge venture. If both the customer and manufacturing contributions were contributed by the American partner, the venture was classified as an American knowledge venture. All other ventures were classified as shared knowledge ventures. The result was 18 Japanese knowledge ventures and 22 shared knowledge ventures. There were no American knowledge ventures.

To support the proposition that the probability of instability increases as the foreign partner acquires local knowledge, the Japanese knowledge ventures should be more unstable. Nine of the unstable ventures were classified as Japanese knowledge ventures and 50 per cent of the Japanese knowledge ventures became unstable as opposed to only 10 per cent of the shared knowledge ventures. A cross-tabulation of the knowledge categories with the stability categories of stable and unstable yielded a significant Chi-square result ($p < 0.05$).

The results suggest that when the Japanese partners had the least to learn in order to compete autonomously, instability often occurred. The results are not meant to suggest that the Japanese partners had a Machiavellian motive in forming their ventures. While several American managers suspected their Japanese partners of having full ownership objectives at the time the ventures were formed, many of the Japanese firms reluctantly entered North America and only at the urging of the Japanese automakers. It is unlikely that these Japanese firms had an initial full ownership goal. If the ventures were formed as a planned stepping stone to full ownership, a relationship between instability and JV equity would be expected. Specifically, the unstable ventures would be more likely to be majority owned by the Japanese partners because, with majority ownership, acquisition of a partner interest is much easier. We found no relationship between equity and instability. Six of the unstable JVs were 50–50 ventures.

The Japanese firms, initially uncertain about operating in North America, seemed to have overestimated the complexity associated with managing a wholly-owned subsidiary in the United States. Several years as part of a JV allowed the firms to acquire the necessary local knowledge to compete autonomously, something they were unable or unwilling to do prior to the JV formation. On the other hand, the American partners may have underestimated the speed by which their Japanese partners could adapt to the North American environment. In the unstable ventures, we found that the American firms formed their ventures with the intention of forging a long-term relationship. Early termination or reorganization of the JVs was not anticipated. However, as the Japanese firms absorbed local knowledge, the American partner's venture role became less important and the balance of power quickly shifted to the Japanese side.

THE VALUE OF LOCAL KNOWLEDGE

Up to this point, we have focused on the effect on JV stability when the foreign partner builds a local knowledge base. An equally important issue is why foreign partners aggressively seek to acquire local knowledge in some JVs while in others, such as Toppan Moore, acquisition does not occur. This question is examined by starting with a key assumption: when a JV is formed, the local knowledge contribution of the local partner has strategic value to the foreign partner. Until the foreign partner acquires local knowledge, the foreign partner will continue to need its local partner.

The foreign partner's valuation of local knowledge involves two stages. The first stage occurs prior to the formation of the JV when the foreign partner considers the value associated with gaining access to a partner's local knowledge. The second stage occurs subsequent to formation. With the JV formed, the foreign partner has access to local knowledge. The question for the foreign partner now becomes: is access sufficient or should the knowledge be acquired? If a high value is attached to knowledge access and acquisition, instability becomes more likely because a foreign partner that is placing a high value on acquisition will not be content with access alone. (We recognize that the local partner contribution can involve more than just local knowledge. The relationship between local partner technology contributions and instability is discussed in the section on controlling instability.)

When the foreign partner has a strategic objective of acquisition and proprietary control over local knowledge, two factors influence the speed of knowledge acquisition.

1 Partner contributions   The extent of local knowledge that must be acquired by a foreign partner to reduce its local partner dependency will be determined by the nature of partner contributions to the JV. Following the classification system used earlier, partner contributions can be classified into three core areas of know-how: manufacturing process and product technology, marketing systems, and infrastructure. Infrastructure incorporates the legal, administrative, and financial aspects of managing the JV.

In the sample of Japanese–American ventures, the Japanese firms quickly built a local knowledge base. In the unstable ventures, Japanese partners generally contributed manufacturing, product, and marketing know-how and relied on their American partners for infrastructure contributions. In a twist on the typical notion of a local market, the Japanese firms, through their transplant connections, often brought 'local' market knowledge from Japan. Thus, the localization task was relatively uncomplicated, involving the acquisition of infrastructure knowledge and the adaptation of existing systems to the United States. Not surprisingly, instability was more likely when local partner contributions were limited to infrastructure knowledge.

In Toppan Moore, Moore contributed manufacturing and product technologies but initially needed its partner for sales and distribution. Over time, the JV modified products to meet the requirements of Japanese customers and developed its own production capabilities, reducing its day-to-day dependence on Moore. At the same time, however, Moore continued to be a formidable research-driven company. While the Japanese partner's immediate operational need for Moore lessened, access to future technological developments remained an important aspect of the relationship. Consequently, the advantages of collaboration for Moore and Toppan Printing continued to outweigh those of competition. In contrast, the Japanese partners in the unstable Japanese–American JVs gave their ventures little autonomy and maintained strict control over manufacturing, product technology, and marketing.

2 The transparency of the local environment   If the environment in which the foreign partner is operating is highly transparent, knowl- edge acquisition will be easier than in a more closed environment. Based on the difficulty Western firms have had in penetrating Japanese markets, and the experience of the Japanese foreign partners in the North America data, the proposition that the United States has a more transparent and accessible environment than Japan appears well-founded.

Regardless of the speed of local knowledge acquisition, it is important to emphasize that when a foreign partner has an explicit learning intent, the local partner is in a vulnerable position. In developing country ventures, the vulnerability of the local partners is particularly acute because the local partner is generally not a competitive threat to the foreign partner outside the JV's country of domicile. Since the foreign partner is usually larger and more international in scope, local partners may be unable to prevent a foreign partner from increasing local knowledge.

In developed country JVs, the local partner may have some leverage over its foreign partner. The partners may be current or potential competitors in each other's home market and may value a stable relationship for competitive reasons. However, if the partner contributions are skewed to the same degree as in the Japanese–American sample, the local partner may have little control over its foreign partner's learning intent.

Access, not acquisition

Despite initially placing a high enough value on the local partner's knowledge to warrant the formation of a JV, the foreign partner may prefer access and stability over acquisition. There are several reasons why a low value may be placed on the acquisition of local knowledge:

- The foreign partner may have an attitude of 'the local partner knows local conditions better than we ever will'.
- The cost of obtaining local knowledge versus the expected payoff. Local market opportunities may be too small and/or uncertain to warrant the learning effort. In the Caribbean JVs this was an important factor contributing to stability.
- The foreign partner may lack the necessary skills to acquire local knowledge. This may be more of an issue for small firms with limited international experience.

If the value of local knowledge declines, in terms of either access or acquisition, the foreign partner may choose to walk away from the venture. A foreign partner that has chosen access rather than acquisition may also, at some point, choose to exercise its option to initiate local knowledge acquisition efforts.

CONTROLLING INSTABILITY

This section considers how managers involved in JVs can develop greater control over instability. To preface the discussion, we again emphasize that stability should not be equated with high performance. As well, stability should not always be the primary JV objective. If learning from a JV partner is an objective, the JV may be seen as transitional. Nonetheless, if managers, and particularly local partner managers, are aware of the factors influencing JV stability they may be able to prevent or control for premature changes in partner relationships.

For a firm interested in maintaining a stable, long-term JV relationship, the Toppan Moore case has several important lessons. One, Moore chose to focus its activities on strengthening the JV itself and building a relationship with its partner, rather than accumulating local country knowledge. Explicit attempts to build local country knowledge by capitalizing on local partner experience are usually transparent and may be interpreted by local partners as competitive rather than collaborative in nature. Two, Moore has been willing to play the role of student and not just teacher, something that many Western firms find difficult.

Moore has learned from its JV and permitted its JV to develop its own culture and systems. Three, continuity in the personal relationships between the top management of both partners was maintained. Without continuity, there is the risk of 'corporate amnesia', whereby managers in the parent companies forget the original alliance motivation and past lessons of the relationship (Turpin 1993).

In the sample of Japanese–American JVs, several American firms recognized the risks associated with the Japanese partner's acquisition of local knowledge and tried to slow their foreign partner's localization efforts. For example, in one case the JV agreement specified that the venture not be allowed to compete directly against the American parent in the domestic automotive business. In another case, the American partner was committed to playing a major role in most facets of JV management. A JV corporate office was established and physically located within the American partner's head office to facilitate an exchange of ideas between American partner and JV personnel.

A local firm may be able to increase the difficulty of learning by the foreign partner. In the sample of Japanese–American JVs, the Japanese firms generally controlled the manufacturing technology, a common situation when market entry is the foreign partner's primary JV objective. If a local partner can establish its technology as an important venture contribution, the foreign partner's learning task will involve more than just local knowledge. As well, the local partner will have a better opportunity of outlearning its foreign partner because its reliance on the foreign partner's technology will be reduced. In the Japanese–American sample, only three JVs were classified as having equal technology contributions from both partners. In the other ventures, the American firms left themselves unprotected because of a reliance on their partner's technology and management of the manufacturing process.

Efforts to limit a foreign partner's learning will not always be successful, especially in an open environment like the United States. For example, in one of the Japanese–American ventures, the American partner wanted to provide the plant manager but the Japanese partner exercised its majority ownership and would not allow it. The American partner provided only one manager to the JV and the Japanese partner explicitly tried to limit the American partner's role in the JV operation. When the JV was terminated prematurely, the Japanese partner established another American plant to develop business with US automakers. In another case, an American partner executive indicated that 'the Japanese partner wanted a foothold in the United States that we could provide. They used us and then threw us away.'

Cultural diversity and stability

Another aspect associated with the control of instability is the cultural diversity of the JV partners. Many articles on JVs have emphasized the problems that occur when firms from different countries form JVs. The presence of societal cultural differences between the partners, it is often argued, contributes to JV instability (Parkhe 1991). Certainly, cultural diversity adds to the difficulty of IJV management. However, our research suggests that the relationship between cultural diversity and stability depends on whether one is viewing stability from the local or foreign partner's perspective.

As a foreign partner gains local experience and builds its local knowledge base, the cultural gap between the foreign and local partners decreases. When that happens JV instability becomes more likely because access to local knowledge was one of the key reasons for forming the JV. Therefore, if the foreign partner does not adapt to the local environment, the diversity between the partners may foster stability.

From the perspective of the local partner adapting to the foreign partner, the situation is somewhat different. If the local partner increases its understanding of its foreign partner's culture, venture stability may increase because the partners have a greater understanding of each other's behaviour. In the sample of Japanese–American JVs, an area that was particularly difficult for American managers to understand was pricing decisions for Japanese customers. Consequently, the pricing structure of JV products was a major source of conflict between the JV partners. Increased understanding by the American partner about its Japanese partner's approach to pricing would potentially eliminate a major source of conflict.

CONCLUSION

When JVs are formed to exploit interfirm differences in skills, there is always the risk that one partner may acquire knowledge that it lacked at the time of alliance formation. When this occurs, the cooperative basis for the JV will erode and venture instability may be the result. When a JV is international and the foreign partner seeks to expand its geographic scope of operations, the local partner's knowledge of economic, political, and cultural environments will be a key contribution to the JV. The main argument in this chapter is that once the venture is formed, if the foreign partner attaches a high value to the acquisition of local knowledge, the probability of JV instability increases. Once a foreign partner has acquired local knowledge, unless the local partner is contributing other valuable and difficult to copy skills to the JV, the rationale for cooperation will be eliminated. Thus, the acquisition of local knowledge is an enabling device for the foreign partner to operate autonomously.

The objective was not to explain JV success as a function of stability. Some ventures are formed as transitional organizational forms, with the partners mutually agreeing on a termination plan. For these ventures, little guidance is offered. Our focus was instability as an undesirable event. Given its undesirability, we argued that if local partners take steps to ensure that their role encompasses more than a local knowledge contribution, instability may be controllable. As well, foreign partners may choose access of local knowledge without acquisition as a viable strategy. Consequently, JVs can be stable and sustainable arrangements for creating competitive advantage. As the Toppan Moore case clearly demonstrates, it can be possible and profitable for a JV to remain stable over a long period.

Chapter 10

Implications and conclusion

This book examined various aspects of IJV management, with an emphasis on how firms can exploit the learning potential in their collaborative ventures. The concluding chapter examines the organizational learning and IJV findings from two theoretical perspectives: resource-based theories of strategy and transaction costs.

LEARNING AND RESOURCE-BASED THEORIES OF STRATEGY

There are several implications for research in the area of firm resources and strategy, an area that is receiving renewed emphasis in the strategy literature.[1] In contrast to the product market positioning frameworks found in the competitive strategy literature, the resource-based view of the firm seeks to understand how organizations accumulate and coordinate internal resources as a means of developing sustainable competitive advantage. Learning is one way for firms to create new resources and skills.

The primary strength of the resource-based view is that complex social phenomena are identified as determinants of core competence and organizational capabilities (Collis 1991: 65). If a strategy is formulated purely from a market positioning perspective, organizational factors associated with its implementation may be ignored. As Porter (1991) observed, firms create and sustain competitive advantage by maintaining a dynamic alignment between strategy and environment and by exploiting unique internal strengths.

JV parents, their perspective of strategy, and learning

The market positioning and resource-based views complement each other and contribute to a more complete view of strategy. The problem facing organizations is that one view may come to predominate, constraining strategic choices and outcomes. Specifically, an organization with an explicit focus on external product markets may not recognize the importance of learning. This was the situation facing many of the American firms studied in this research. These firms had explicit learning objectives but were implementing their JV strategies from a narrow market positioning orientation. Because of an inability to abandon a preoccupation with transplant market access as a means of displacing lost domestic markets, many American firms had unsuccessful learning experiences. Had the firms focused on the potential JV benefits in terms of enhanced skills and competencies, which is consistent with a learning objective, the learning outcomes would have been significantly different.

Table 10.1 demonstrates how the perspectives of competition and strategy adopted by JV parents can have an impact on their ability to exploit learning opportunities. Quadrant 1 shows defensive (i.e. 'we better form a JV before it is too late') JV objectives coupled with a market positioning view. This can lead to a short-term focus designed to protect a domestic market position. Quadrant 2 suggests that a market position view with an offensive venture strategy can result in a longer-term focus on product line expansion, possibly in both domestic and international markets. In quadrants 1 and 2, the JV parents will probably view stability as a reasonable indicator of JV success. In the context of this study, a stability objective is inherently flawed. In the long term, the Japanese partners may not need their American partners once they learn to operate in North America. Unless the structure of the automotive industry changes dramatically from its current state, many American firms will remain dependent on their Japanese partners for market access purposes.

Quadrant 3 indicates a resource-based perspective associated with defensive JV objectives. Learning in this situation is focused on migratory knowledge rather than the complex embedded knowledge of the JV partner. Quadrant 4 represents the most desirable state: an offensive approach to the JV directed by a resource-based view of strategy. When learning is a collaborative objective, the termination of an agreement should not be seen as evidence of failure (Hamel 1991). In cases of JV termination (but not necessarily dissolution), the parent firm gaining full ownership may have outlearned its former partner. In all but one case of termination in this study, the Japanese partner acquired full ownership of the JV business and appeared willing to make a long-term commitment to its new subsidiary. The American firms, on the other hand, generally saw termination as evidence of JV failure.

Table 10.1 Strategic perspective and learning

Parent's JV objectives	Parent's strategic perspective	
	Market positioning	*Resource-based*
Defensive ('have to')	1 Short-term focus; joint venture is a stand-alone profit centre; primary objective is to protect domestic market position	3 Medium-term focus; learning focus on migratory knowledge; reducing partner dependence not a primary objective
Offensive ('want to')	2 Medium-term focus; primary objective is to expand product line, improve domestic and international market positions	4 Long-term focus; erasing partner dependency is an objective; create value by appropriating partner skills

The situation of the Japanese partners is also interesting, especially in the cases of JV termination. The Japanese firms that acquired full ownership of the JV businesses were able to apply their newly internalized skills to compete autonomously in North America, something that they were unable or unwilling to do prior to the JV formation. An evaluation of the strategy of these firms solely from a product-market positioning perspective would fail to recognize that performance is contingent on product-market positioning factors and the ability to acquire the necessary organizational skills to compete in a new market.

In sum, the finding that firms were using their JVs as learning vehicles is consistent with the argument that firms seeking to improve their competitive position cannot ignore learning and organization skill-building (Bettis *et al.* 1992). From this perspective, current market position provides only one measure of competitiveness because it is focused on product-based advantages at a given point in time. Without the ability to innovate and change quickly, achieving sustainable competitive advantage will not be possible.

Imperfect imitability

For firm resources to hold the potential for sustained competitive advantage, they must have several attributes (Barney 1991; Grant 1991).

Among those attributes is imperfect imitability, which occurs when resources possessed by one firm cannot be obtained by another firm. The failure of many American firms to exploit successfully their JV learning opportunities can be traced, in part, to their inability to imitate the strategies of their Japanese partners. There are several factors contributing to imperfect imitability; of particular interest for this study are the concepts of causal ambiguity and social complexity.

Causal ambiguity arises when managers do not understand the relationship between organizational actions and outcomes (Reed and DeFillippi 1990). Grant (1991: 125) observed that 'if a firm wishes to imitate the strategy of a rival, it must first establish the capabilities which underlie the rival's competitive advantage, and then it must determine what resources are required to replicate these capabilities'.

The findings of this study support the notion of causal ambiguity as an impediment to the imitation of successful firm strategies. For JV and alliance-learning strategies to be viable and for potential learning opportunities to be recognized, firms must overcome the ambiguity associated with their partner's areas of competency. However, many American parents were searching for the key to a Japanese mystique rather than trying to develop a fundamental understanding of the link between the Japanese partner's resources and its underlying competitive advantage.

The automotive JVs in this study should have provided the necessary access for American firms to overcome the sources of ambiguity associated with Japanese partner competencies. Many JVs were established as virtual clones of the Japanese partners, giving the American partner unhindered access to the dedicated assets of their partners. Despite this access, learning often proved to be a difficult experience, suggesting that having information is not the same as understanding it. Chapter 7 indicated that the learning emphasis of the American firms was often on visible firm differences rather than on complex tacit knowledge. Instead of finding migratory knowledge, American firms encountered differences that were embedded in the routines of their partners. As Badaracco (1991: 80) explained, 'The main difficulty in understanding the challenge of embedded knowledge is that it requires rethinking familiar ideas about firms, their boundaries, and the work of business managers.'

Social complexity is a second attribute of imperfect imitability identified by Barney (1991). This occurs when firm resources are complex social phenomena that firms cannot systematically manage and influence. This study provides evidence that social complexity can have an important influence on the process of learning and imitation.

One factor that was particularly difficult for American managers to comprehend was the role and implications of Japanese networks. This issue was examined in detail in Chapter 3. The American firms generally recognized that there were competitive implications associated with the Japanese network of relationships, especially those between suppliers and manufacturers. However, there was often incomplete understanding of the specific factors that enabled the Japanese firms to exploit the network relationships for competitive advantage.

Transferability

Even if the barrier of imperfect imitability can be overcome, successful learning by imitation requires internalization of the skills and capabilities of another firm (Grant 1991). This requires specific efforts to transfer and accumulate new resources and organizational knowledge. This study broke new ground by attempting to measure the learning efforts of JV parents. The results indicated that a successful learning strategy requires various different actions designed to channel knowledge from the JV to the parent.

The study also found that learning efforts alone cannot overcome a lack of receptivity to learning at the parent level. The strategic relationship between the parent and its JV is a key aspect of receptivity. This relationship is important because while specific learning efforts may be put into place, without an attempt to integrate parent and JV strategies, mobility of the new skills and capabilities will be constrained.

JVs, LEARNING, AND TRANSACTION COSTS

Transaction cost explanations for the formation of JVs provide a compelling economic rationale for the formation of JVs and, in particular, for the superiority of the JV mode of organization under specific circumstances (Hennart 1988; Kogut 1988). However, the transaction costs perspective is restrictive because it neglects more behavioural issues and implies too strongly a tractable economic analysis in understanding cooperative relationships.

Hennart (1991: 495) proposed that firms form JVs when they need to combine with other firms intermediate inputs that are subject to high market transaction costs. One of the inputs that firms might seek is tacit or embedded knowledge for which there is no reliable market. Thus, as Shan (1990) maintained, the organizational learning perspective may be consistent with a transaction cost argument because of the absence of a market for tacit knowledge. The difficulty with applying transaction cost theory to the learning perspective is the unit of analysis. Transaction cost analysis is primarily focused on single transactions as units of analysis (Doz and Prahalad 1991). However, the ambiguous nature of embedded knowledge and organizational skills makes it unlikely that identifiable units for these goods can be operationally delineated.

From a learning perspective, the unit of analysis begins with the individual manager, proceeding to an examination of how managerial knowledge acquisition and interpretation are integrated into shared understanding at the organization level. In the JV situation, the important question involves how knowledge generated within the JV is transferred and integrated by the parent. Therefore, the process of learning along with the nature of its outcome takes precedence over the choice of a structural mode by which to exploit the learning opportunity. In this research, many American firms experienced great difficulty in exploiting learning opportunities despite having access to the embedded skills of their partners. Consequently, an analysis of the transaction costs associated with acquiring the embedded knowledge via a marketplace alternative may be of limited usefulness.

Finally, for the JVs in this study, transaction cost theory is limited in its ability to explain Japanese firms' choice between full ownership and JVs. In many cases, the Japanese partners were 'encouraged' by their Japanese customers to locate in North America. Refusing to follow the Japanese automakers to North America would have risked damaging what Kester (1991) called the intricate network of implicit reciprocal trading agreements that exists in Japan between suppliers and manufacturers. The Japanese automakers played a role in JV formation decisions because using JV suppliers may have helped alleviate some of the political concerns about screwdriver auto plants in the United States (Womack 1988). Thus, for many Japanese suppliers, a primary consideration in both the decision to invest in North America and the choice of the JV mode was the desire to maintain an existing supplier–manufacturer relationship. This desire to maintain relationship goodwill is not explained by a transaction cost framework.

In sum, transaction cost theory provides useful input toward understanding issues of ownership choice. However, the view of this study, and consistent with Kogut's (1988) argument, is that the explanatory factors underlying the learning perspective are organizational and cognitive, and only indirectly economically motivated. Because organizational knowledge often has definite tacit and learning-by-doing dimensions, a rational economic analysis of the learning process and mode of knowledge transfer may not be possible (Teece 1982).

CONCLUSION

Clearly, there are many issues associated with the management of IJVs that require further research and, in particular, further theoretical exploration is necessary. The issues examined in this book, such as control, performance, and learning, are sure to remain important as firms wrestle with the complexity of managing collaborative relationships.

The primary focus of the book was on learning and JVs. As a contribution to the organizational learning literature, this research highlights how learning dissipates as it moves from individual interpretation to group integration and finally institutionalization at the organizational level. Many questions remain about the inter-relationships among the levels of learning and in particular the feedback loops. Future research needs to address how institutionalized learning impacts new interpretation and integration, and how shared understanding in terms of integrated learning impacts the development of new and perhaps different insights.

This research also raises the issue of learning how to learn as a competitive advantage. It has been suggested that Japanese firms are more adept than Western firms at maximizing learning opportunities (Hedlund and Nonaka 1993). In a Japanese firm in Hamel's (1991) study, managers indicated they were not worried about disclosing what they had learned. These managers were so confident in their ability to learn that they knew they would always be one step ahead of their partner. In this regard, it is important to recognize that it is the rate of learning and not just the learning itself that is important. When the complexity associated with the rate of learning is added to the learning equation, it is clear that there are many further issues to address, since many of the companies studied had difficulty recognizing learning opportunities, let alone exploiting them.

To conclude, this book examined various issues associated with IJV management. The exploration of organizational learning highlighted the complexity of the phenomenon and illustrated that the important issues in organization learning span organization levels, which means the issues also span research boundaries. As international competition intensifies, the efficiency and extent of learning by organizations may become the essential factor that determines long-term competitive success. Learning through alliances and IJVs provides an important platform for achieving that success.

Appendix

Research methodology

This book draws on several sources of data. In this Appendix, the two primary studies are discussed as stages one and two. The first stage used a field-based survey designed

1 to examine the characteristics of Japanese JVs in North America, with a particular emphasis on the 'Japanese' context;
2 to provide contextual understanding of the alliance learning issues;
3 to gain a cross-sectional perspective on the basic dimensions of alliance learning.

The second stage was aimed at understanding in more detail the learning process that emerged in stage one. This stage used an open-ended approach of grounded theory building (Glaser and Strauss 1967). Chapters 2, 3, 4 and 9 draw primarily on stage one data. Chapters 6, 7, and 8 use data from both stages.

In addition to the two stages of research, additional data sources used in Chapters 4 and 9 are discussed in the respective chapters.

STAGE ONE: A SURVEY OF JVs

This research stage incorporated multiple methods of data collection and analysis. A multimethod design helped address the concerns raised by Parkhe (1993). Parkhe argued that international JV research has employed methods that are unlikely to yield advances in theory. To move JV theory past its current evolutionary stage, researchers were encouraged to progress through stages of exploratory, descriptive, and finally explanatory research. Parkhe further argued that it is unlikely that the more process-oriented aspects of interfirm cooperation can be satisfactorily studied using currently emphasized 'hard' methods of research.[1]

An advantage of multimethod research is the ability to collect various types of data (Brewer and Hunter 1989). For this research stage, both interview and questionnaire data were collected via a field study. In conducting field-based research with an interview component, cost and logistics factors limit sample size. However, the research objectives for this study required an understanding of various organizational processes that could not be captured using a questionnaire exclusively and, therefore, access to qualitative data was considered an essential element. Thus, it was concluded that a combination of questionnaire and interview methods would allow an efficient and systematic approach to the research problem and provide a foundation of descriptive realism (Lee 1991).

All JVs in the sample competed in the automotive supply industry. Using a single industry with a homogeneous set of organizations imposes certain constraints. In particular, theory development is restricted to limited domain or middle-range theories (Pinder and Moore 1980) and generalizability is confined to other industries sharing similar structural characteristics. However, a single industry offers greater control over market and environmental peculiarities, an important consideration in exploratory research.

The development of the research sample involved several steps. First, a Toronto-based organization called Pacific Automotive Cooperation (PAC) was contacted. PAC's mission is to introduce North American and Japanese JV partners and to promote Japanese investment. PAC monitors and tracks Japanese automobile-related investment in North America. PAC provided a list of Japanese–North American JVs involved in the manufacture of automotive parts (such as brakes, mufflers, and seats), and automotive materials (such as glass and paint).

Next, qualifying JVs were identified from the PAC list of JVs. Several organizational attributes were considered important for the sample. For logistical reasons, the geographic scope of the JVs was restricted to Ontario, the United States Midwest (Ohio, Michigan, Illinois, and Indiana) and the United States Upper South (Kentucky and Tennessee). The number of partners was held to two because of the complexity of ventures with more than two partners. Each partner had an equity interest of at least 20 per cent. The start of JV operations was no earlier than 1985 and no later than January 1990. To ensure completeness, the PAC list of qualifying JVs was supplemented with a review of automotive supplier firm activities covered in the trade journal *Ward's Auto World* and also a review of regional business publications in *UMI's Business Dateline*. In total, 54 qualifying ventures were identified.

Managers in the JVs were contacted via letter and telephone. Three JVs did not qualify for the study. Overall, 42 of 51 qualifying JVs participated in the study and two cases were later eliminated when informants were unable to provide sufficient data. Interviews were conducted with 51 JV managers and 7 parent managers. With one exception, interviews were conducted in person in the informants' offices. Total interview time per scheduled interview ranged from one hour to more than four hours, with an average of two hours. All follow-up interviews, carried out for about one third of the cases, were done by telephone.

The key informants for the interviews and questionnaires were the senior American managers in the ventures. These managers, usually the JV general managers or presidents, were chosen for several reasons. One, Cohen and Levinthal (1990: 132) argued that learning capacity is strongly influenced by the individuals who stand at the interface between sub-units within the firm or at the interface with the environment. In a JV, presidents and general managers perform this interface role and therefore represent the primary conduit for the transfer of knowledge between the JV and the parent. Two, as the managers at the interface between the parent and the JV partner, these managers were very knowledgeable about partner relationships and a reliable source of data (Geringer and Hebert 1991). Three, as the senior American managers in the JVs, these managers would probably be knowledgeable about organizational processes and could assess the importance of processes from a strategic perspective. Finally, given the sensitivity of the information, JV managers were expected to be (and were) more cooperative than more senior managers at the American parent level.

Interview process

The interviews followed a semistructured format based on an interview guide. There was both an open-ended sequence of questions and a focused set of questions designed to measure specific variables. The open-ended questions allowed theory development to be grounded in the experiences and terminology of organizational participants (recommended by Beyer and Trice 1982). Descriptive data produced by the open-ended questions were also important for exploring proposed relationships (see Table A.1 for examples of the open-ended interview questions).

For all interview data, data reduction began immediately following the interview and helped bring the raw data into a manageable form. Within a 24-hour period, the detailed interview write-ups were

Table A.1 Interview questions

Examples of the open-ended questions that provided structure to the interviews:

1 Describe the formation of the JV: why was it formed; how did the two partners get together; which partner initiated the JV? Were the partners involved in prior relationships before the formation of the JV?

2 What were the Japanese partner's motives in forming the JV? How would you evaluate the contribution of the Japanese partner to the JV? Is the Japanese partner's managerial contribution critical to the success of the JV?

3 What role did the transplant customers play in the JV formation?

4 Was access to the Japanese partner's skills and knowledge an important consideration (for the American partner) in forming the JV?

5 How much operational autonomy does the JV have: from its American parent? from its Japanese parent? Which partner has the most influence on the management of the JV?

6 How would you describe the relationship between the partners? Do the partners agree on the time frame for profitability?

7 Are the parents satisfied with the JV's performance? Has the JV met the American parent's expectations?

8 How do the transplant customers influence the management of the JV?

completed. The interview write-ups summarized the interviews in a consistent and logical manner. The main objective of the write-ups was a 'product intelligible to anyone, not just the fieldworker' (Miles and Huberman 1984: 50). All write-ups were reviewed for omissions and clarity problems with follow-up data collected if necessary.

As the research progressed the categorized data and write-ups were examined for emerging patterns, themes, and processes that might account for the frequency and absence or presence of data categories. An objective of exploratory research is the discovery of new categories of data that emerge out of the data rather than having been decided prior to data collection and analysis (Patton 1987). For example, a pattern that emerged early in the study was a relationship between JV performance and knowledge management.

Research variables

Learning intent was operationally defined as the strength of the American parent's JV learning objective. The cases were classified into three categories: no intent, moderate intent, and strong intent, based on information provided by the informant. As a basis for making the classification I looked for several forms of evidence. I examined the history of the venture and the original formation objectives and probed for insights on the nature of the learning intent. Was the focus on manufacturing process technology, product technology, or a more general category of 'managerial' know-how? As Huber and Power (1985: 176–177) recommended with respect to retrospective reports, I applied several other guidelines for eliciting valid data, including the assurance of anonymity and confidentiality, pretesting the interview methods, and establishing a contract with the informants to provide feedback on study results.

As a test of the convergent validity of the learning intent classifications, the questionnaire included the question 'How much do you agree with the following statement: One of the North American partner's objectives in forming the JV was to learn something, e.g. an unfamiliar market, technology, or management technique?' (7-point scale, ranging from 'strongly disagree' to 'strongly agree'). The learning intent measure, with the three classifications used as rankings, correlated positively with the questionnaire responses ($r = 0.30, p < 0.05$).[2]

Parent experience with JVs was evaluated as a dichotomous variable. I did not distinguish between international or domestic JV experience for the reason that either type of venture should be an important source of managerial experience. For prior experience with the JV partner, I looked for evidence that the partner firms had worked together in a cooperative relationship such as technology sharing or licensing arrangement. If the relationship was a one-time interaction or a supplier–customer relationship, the case was coded as no prior relationship.

Performance was measured using both questionnaire and interview data. The interview measure is discussed in Chapter 2 and the questionnaire measure is discussed in Chapter 4. Trust, openness, and strategic centrality were evaluated using questionnaire data. Table A.2 shows the items for the questionnaire measures. The trust measure drew on the study by Anderson and Narus (1990) of marketing channel partnerships

Table A.2 Scale items

Performance:

1 The North American parent is satisfied with the performance of the JV.
2 The partners work together so that both can benefit from the JV.
3 The efforts of the partners are consistent with the objectives of the JV.
4 The JV has met the objectives for which it was established.

Trust:

1 The Japanese partner is a firm that stands by its word.
2 There is a high level of trust in the working relationship between the partners.
3 The North American partner can rely on its partner to abide by the JV management agreement.

Openness:

1 Both partners willingly share information with each other.
2 The relationship between the JV partners is open and informal.
3 The Japanese partner willingly shares information.

Strategic centrality:

1 JV managers regularly communicate with managers from the head office of the North American partner.
2 JV managers involve managers from the head office of the North American partner in JV decisions.
3 The JV operates independently of the JV board (reverse coded).
4 The JV board provides the only way for senior managers of the partner firms to become involved in JV activities (reverse coded).

---

and Beamish (1984). The measure had three items with a Cronbach's alpha of 0.84.

Partner openness was measured using a new scale developed for this research. The measure is based on Gupta's (1987) notion that openness involves the sharing of information across organizational boundaries. A three-item scale with an alpha of 0.83 was used.

Following Shortell and Zajac (1988), a four-item scale with an alpha of 0.73 was developed to measure strategic centrality. This measure is similar to the measure of project commitment used by Beamish (1984). As a test of construct validity for strategic centrality, a measure of communication intensity between the JV and its American parent was developed. As anticipated, the correlation between strategic centrality and intensity of communication between JV and parent managers was positive and significant ($r = 0.59$, $p < 0.001$).

STAGE TWO: CASE STUDY

Stage one of the research confirmed the existence of important learning opportunities for the American JV parents and provided the foundation for an emerging model of alliance learning. Various parent learning efforts were identified. A linkage between JV performance and learning emerged. The second stage of research was aimed at understanding in more detail the learning process that emerged in stage one. An emphasis on process suggested the need for a longitudinal approach that provided deeper and more extensive access to the individuals involved in collaborative exchange.

Five cases from the initial set of JVs were selected for further analysis. Several criteria were used to select the cases, with the objective of finding variance across several dimensions. Of particular interest was the learning potential created by the JVs. This factor was important because it influenced the learning efforts initiated by the JV parents and the motivation of the American parents to exploit the learning potential. Differences in JV performance, partner history, and the source of JV management were other criteria used in the selection of cases (see Table A.3 for case selection criteria). As well, the JVs selected were still in existence because it is generally better to initiate historical study before the outcomes of strategic change processes become known (Van de Ven 1992).

JV performance was evaluated from the perspective of the American parent and was based on the American parent's overall satisfaction with performance. To evaluate JV skill differences, JV manufacturing and overall performance relative to the American parent was considered. Note that in each of the cases, the JV product line was functionally similar to the American parent product line. In the absence of product similarity, evaluating skill differences becomes more difficult. I looked for evidence that the JV was exceeding the parent's quality efforts because this was an indication of partner skill differences at the manufacturing process level. Other skills, such as marketing, distribution, and product design were also considered. Partner history reflects the extent of previous collaborative relationships between the partners. Learning efforts initiated are based on the stage one results. JV management indicates if senior JV management came from the American parent or if outsiders were hired.

Table A.3 Case characteristics

	A	B	C	D	E
JV performance	low	medium	high	medium	high
JV skill differences	high	medium	medium	high	low
Partner history	none	limited	limited	extensive	none
Learning efforts initiated	limited	moderate	extensive	extensive	moderate
JV management	outside	parent	parent	parent	parent

The interviews in this stage were usually 1.5 to 2 hours in length, although a few were half day or more. As in the first research stage, data reduction began immediately following the interview, with the objective of bringing the raw data into a manageable form. An analysis activity that occurred throughout this research stage (and the previous one) was the development of analytic memoranda. This process, called 'memoing' by Glaser (1978), involved the recording of conceptual and analytic impressions as they occurred. The impressions reflected several different themes, including the preliminary identification of patterns, summaries of unique or surprising site attributes, and ideas on data analysis. Included in the interview write-ups was a separate section called 'researcher's general impressions' (Bourgeois and Eisenhardt 1988). In this section, emerging thoughts about the conceptual framework were summarized as they related to the particular interview site and also unique ideas about the site.

Notes

2 JAPANESE JVs: CHARACTERISTICS AND PERFORMANCE

1 Although there were several Canadian firms in the sample, for brevity, future references to the sample of firms use American rather than North American.

2 The apparent reluctance of the Japanese transplants to use local suppliers became a major political issue in Japanese–United States trade negotiations. The transplants argue that North American suppliers were unable to meet their product quality, design, engineering, and delivery demands. Not surprisingly, the North American suppliers tended to reject this argument. This study found almost unanimous agreement from the JV managers that the products manufactured in the JVs were far superior to those manufactured by the American parents.

3 Womack (1988) reported that within its supplier group Toyota decided which of its suppliers should form JVs and which should form wholly-owned subsidiaries.

4 Although a Japanese customer does have substantial leverage over its supplier, the network of cross shareholdings and implicit expectations is such that outright abuses of the system are relatively uncommon (Kester 1991).

5 Because of their reliance on outsourcing, Japanese transplants have frequently been called 'screwdriver plants' in which the value added is limited to assembly operations.

6 Beamish (1988) developed the notion of mutual need, which may apply to cases where a single initiator could not be identified.

7 It is important to emphasize that longevity is not always a JV objective. Premature JV termination may be a mutual decision or it may be precipitated by the actions of one partner. This issue is considered in detail in Chapter 9.

8 As a manager explained, 'A big misconception is that Japanese have long horizons and Americans have short horizons. The Japanese horizon can be long or it can be short, it depends on the issue. If the issue is profit the Japanese partner will often take a long-term view. If the issue is quality and productivity the Japanese partner will want to act very quickly. They will bring over engineers and technical people and do what ever it takes to solve quality problems.'

3 THE ROLE OF JAPANESE NETWORKS

1 For detailed analyses of Japanese networks and enterprise systems, see Fruin (1992) and Gerlach (1992b).

2 For an examination of a Japanese primary manufacturer's reliance on its suppliers, see Smitka (1991). Smitka focused on Diamond Star Motors (DSM), the JV between Chrysler and Mitsubishi. DSM, taken over by Mitsubishi, was formed to assemble a Japanese-designed car in the United States.

3 This is not to suggest that financial factors were totally irrelevant to the Japanese firms. The point is that the network relationship was also a critical factor and, in many cases, the most important factor. To support this argument, several informants indicated that the Japanese partner, given a choice, would have chosen to remain in Japan and export parts to North America.

4 Several managers commented that the Japanese companies were surprised by the level of competition between Japanese companies in North America. The explanation may be that, once out of Japan, firms are more aggressive and less inclined to play the role of pliable supplier. If there are new plants in Japan, they probably operate within the normal operating code. In the words of a JV president, 'Now, with all the new plants and potential business in America, nobody wants to risk missing a piece of the action. So they [the Japanese suppliers] all come over even if they don't have any guarantee of getting the business.'

5 Cusumano and Takeishi (1991) provide an excellent overview of Japanese automaker pricing practices.

6 In 1992, changes were made in US antitrust enforcement policies that may bring foreign firm conduct outside the United States within US jurisdiction. There has been speculation that these changes were aimed at *keiretsu* activities.

4 THE CONTROL AND PERFORMANCE OF INTERNATIONAL JVs

1 Although Blodgett (1992) maintained that her measure of instability was not an indicator of performance, she also argued that her findings supported the results of Beamish and Banks (1987) on the control–performance question.

2 Looking at control over specific activities suggests that control may be split, as opposed to shared. Shared control, as discussed by Killing (1983), means that the partners share in the decision-making of the venture. Split control is somewhat different in that each partner has a realm of control and neither partner has overall control (Geringer and Hebert 1989). The concept of bargaining power examined in this chapter has many similarities to the notion of split control. Complete bargaining power will generally not rest with one partner; in most cases, power will be distributed or split on the basis of various determinants.

3 Horaguchi (1991) compared the Ministry of Finance survey and the Toyo Keizai survey and concluded that the Toyo Kezai survey was a reliable source of FDI data.

4 The JV's management style provides some evidence as to overall JV control. However, management style is primarily concerned with operational activities whereas control deals with strategic areas of the business. As an indication of the links between style and control, of the 18 shared management ventures, 13 were classified as hybrid management style ventures. Of the 20 Japanese dominant ventures, 10 were classified as Japanese management style ventures.

5 Using the three-category interview-based measure of partner satisfaction discussed in Chapter 2, Hypotheses 1 and 2 were not supported. For Hypothesis 3, a chi-square test indicated a relationship between customer dominance and satisfaction (chi-square = 8.49, $p < 0.05$)

5 COLLABORATION AND LEARNING: CONCEPTUAL BACKGROUND

1 Huber (1991) noted that the terms information and knowledge have been used somewhat interchangeably in the organizational learning literature. This issue is examined in Chapter 7.

2 There has been only limited empirical investigation of these concepts; consequently, little is known about how organizations and their managers interpret equivocal events.

3 Along a similar vein, Ghemawat (1991) suggested that strategy reflects irreversible commitments made under conditions of uncertainty.

4 Some information may emerge that is new to all JV partners and, therefore, does not originate with a specific partner. However, if both partners make specific contributions to the JV, the information of interest to a 'learning' organization will probably be associated with the skills and capabilities of a JV partner.

6 DIMENSIONS SHAPING THE LEARNING PROCESS

1 Managers usually focused on superior quality. In several cases the superior quality clearly had a higher cost.

2 Qualitative data classifications were done independently of the questionnaire data.

3 However, March et al. (1991: 6) described organizational learning as involving a balance between stable, shared knowledge and the exploration of novel ideas. Stable knowledge may interfere with the discovery of contrary experience while novel ideas may interfere with the maintenance and sharing of interpretation.

4 The JVs were classified on the basis of their product strategy relative to the American parent. Two categories were used: same product and different product. Openness was higher for JVs with products new to the American firm (5.62 vs. 4.67, $t = 2.61$, $p < 0.05$).

7 A MULTI-LEVEL FRAMEWORK OF ORGANIZATIONAL LEARNING

1 Weick discussed 'believing is seeing' and suggested that beliefs are cause maps that 'people impose on the world after which they see what they have already imposed' (1979: 135). This argument suggests that organizational learning will be shaped and constrained by an existing set of managerial beliefs.

2 The influence of JV performance (the performance measurement is discussed in Chapter 2) on learning is supported by the positive relationships between performance and learning efforts ($r = 0.52$, $p < 0.01$) and performance. This suggests that firms satisfied with performance took a more active interest in capitalizing on learning opportunities.

9 LEARNING AND JV STABILITY

1 For a more detailed analysis, see Beamish and Makino (1992).

2 The Caribbean JVs were first studied in the early 1980s. For detailed reports on the initial study see Beamish (1988) and Beamish and Banks (1987). Initial data collection, conducted in 1982, involved 66 JVs located in 27 developing countries. Included in the study were 12 comparative core cases, of which 7 were located in one Caribbean country. These 7 JVs were the basis for data used in the current study. One of the 7 ventures had been terminated after a change of ownership at the parent level and the introduction of a policy against minority-owned JVs. In a second venture, local partner ownership became very dispersed, making it difficult to identify local partners with management interests. This left 5 of the core cases still in existence (although by our definition of stability, the other 2 by one overriding question: why had these JVs survived? The data collection involved interviews in 1990 with the JV general managers based in the Caribbean country (plus a senior parent manager in one case) and replication of a questionnaire used in the original study. The questionnaire focused on issues of JV formation, control, and performance.

The original data collection was restricted to JVs in two industrial sectors. All cases were manufacturers and in 1982 had been in operation a minimum of three years. In 1990, the JVs ranged in age from 15 to 25 years. In one case the foreign partner had majority ownership, in two cases the foreign partner had 50 per cent ownership, and in two cases the foreign partner had less than 50 per cent ownership.

3 A seldom used option is to incorporate 'fade-out' provisions in the JV agreement. This type of venture has only been used for any length of time in China and even there has been largely discontinued. Another option where longevity is not a goal is to use 'contractual' JVs.

4 Interviews were conducted with various managers including a Moore Corp. division president, the Toppan Printing managing director, and the Japanese president of the JV. Interviews in Japan were conducted in Japanese and both the Japanese and Canadian managers participating in the study verified the detailed case write-up. As an example of an enduring relationship, the

question raised was why had this JV remained stable when many other Western–Japanese ventures in Japan were being terminated. This case study generated our proposition regarding the direct relationship between instability and the foreign partner's knowledge of local market, political, and cultural conditions.

10 IMPLICATIONS AND CONCLUSION

1 For example, see Barney (1991), Burgelman and Rosenbloom (1989), Nelson (1991), and Rumelt et al. (1991).

APPENDIX: RESEARCH METHODOLOGY

1 Although various challenges to large sample quantitative research methods have been made over the past few decades, critics of 'hard' research have become more vocal. Besides Parkhe (1993), see Bettis (1991) and Schwenk and Dalton (1991).
2 Qualitative data classifications were done independently of the questionnaire data.

Bibliography

Abbeglen, J.C. and Stalk, G. (1985) *Kaisha: The Japanese Corporation*, New York: Basic Books.

Aguilar, F.J. (1967) *Scanning the Business Environment*, New York: Macmillan.

Anderson, E. (1990) 'Two firms, one frontier: On assessing JV performance', *Sloan Management Review* 18 (Winter): 19–30.

Anderson, J.C. and Narus, J.A. (1990) 'A model of distributor firm and manufacturer firm working partnerships', *Journal of Marketing* 54, 1: 42–58.

Aoki, M. (1990) 'Toward an economic model of the Japanese firm', *Journal of Economic Literature* 28 (March): 1–27.

Argyris, C. and Schon, D.A. (1978) *Organization Learning: A Theory of Action Perspective*, Reading, MA: Addison-Wesley Publishing Co.

Bacharach, S. and Lawler, E.J. (1980) *Power and Politics in Organizations*, San Francisco: Jossey-Bass.

Badaracco, J.L. (1991) *The Knowledge Link*, Boston: Harvard Business School Press.

Barney, J. (1991) 'Firm resources and sustained competitive advantage', *Journal of Management* 17: 99–120.

Bartlett, C.A. and Ghoshal, S. (1989) *Managing Across Borders: The Transnational Solution*, Boston: Harvard Business School Press.

Beamish, P.W. (1984) *Joint Venture Performance in Developing Countries*, unpublished Ph.D. diss., University of Western Ontario.

—— (1985) 'The characteristics of joint ventures in developed and developing countries', *Columbia Journal of World Business* 20 (Fall): 13–19.

—— (1988) *Multinational JVs in Developing Countries*, London: Routledge.

Beamish, P.W. and Banks, J.C. (1987) 'Equity JVs and the theory of the multinational enterprise', *Journal of International Business Studies* 18 (Summer): 1–16.

Beamish, P.W. and Makino, S. (1992) *Toppan Moore*, Western Business School case no. 9-92-G001.

Bettis, R.A. (1991) 'Strategic management and the straitjacket: An editorial essay', *Organization Science* 2: 315–319.

Bettis, R.A., Bradley, S.P., and Hamel, G. (1992) 'Outsourcing and industrial decline', *Academy of Management Executive* 6: 7–22.

Beyer, J.M. and Trice, H.M. (1982) 'The utilization process: A conceptual framework and synthesis of empirical literature', *Administrative Science Quarterly* 27: 591–622.

Blau, P.M. (1964) *Exchange and Power in Social Life*, New York: Wiley.

Bleeke, J. and Ernst, D. (1991) 'The way to win in cross-border alliances', *Harvard Business Review* 69, 6: 127–135.

Blodgett, L.L. (1992) 'Factors in the instability of international JVs: An event history analysis', *Strategic Management Journal* 13: 475–481.

Borys, B. and Jemison, D.B. (1989) 'Hybrid arrangements as strategic alliances: Theoretical issues in organizational combinations', *Academy of Management Review* 14: 234–249.

Bourgeois, L.J. and Eisenhardt, K. (1988) 'Strategic decision processes in high velocity environments', *Management Science* 34: 816–835.

Brewer, J. and Hunter, A. (1989) *Multimethod Research: A Synthesis of Styles*, Newbury Park, CA: Sage.

Brown, J.S. and Duguid, P. (1991) 'Organizational learning and communities of practice: Towards a unified view of working, learning, and organization', *Organization Science* 2: 40–57.

Burgelman, R.A. and Rosenbloom, R.S. (1989) 'Technology strategy: An evolutionary process perspective', in R. Rosenbloom and R. Burgelman (eds) *Research on Technological Innovation, Management, and Policy*, volume 4, Greenwich, CT: JAI Press.

Chandler, A.D., Jr. (1962) *Strategy and Structure: Chapters in the History of the Industrial Enterprise*, Cambridge, MA: MIT Press.

Cohen, M.D. and Sproull, L.S. (1991) 'Editor's introduction', *Organization Science* 2.

Cohen, W.M. and Levinthal, D.A. (1990) 'Absorptive capacity: A new perspective on learning and innovation', *Administrative Science Quarterly* 35: 128–152.

Collis, D.J. (1991) 'A resource-based analysis of global competition: The case of the bearings industry', *Strategic Management Journal* 12 (Special Issue): 49–68.

Contractor, F.C. and Lorange, P. (1988) 'Why should firms cooperate? The strategy and economics basis for cooperative ventures', in F. Contractor and P. Lorange (eds) *Cooperative Strategies in International Business*, Toronto: Lexington Books.

Cusumano, M. and Takeishi, A. (1991) 'Supplier relations and management: A survey of Japanese-transplant and US auto plants', *Strategic Management Journal* 12: 563–588.

Cutts, R.L. (1992) 'Capitalism in Japan: Cartels and keiretsu', *Harvard Business Review* 70, 4: 48–55.

Cyert, R.M. and March, J.G. (1963) *A Behavioral Theory of the Firm*, Englewood Cliffs, NJ: Prentice Hall.

Daft, R.L. and Weick, K.E. (1984) 'Towards a model of organizations as interpretation systems', *Academy of Management Review* 9: 284–295.

De Geus, A.P. (1988) 'Planning as learning', *Harvard Business Review* 66, 2: 70–74.

Dodgson, M. (1993) 'Learning, trust, and technological collaboration', *Human Relations* 46: 77–95.

Dodwell Marketing Consultants (1990) *The Structure of the Japanese Auto Parts Industry*, Tokyo: Dodwell Marketing Consultants.

Doyle, P., Saunders, J., and Wong, V. (1992) 'Competition in global markets: A case study of American and Japanese competition in the British market', *Journal of International Business Studies* 23: 419–442.

Doz, Y.L. and Prahalad, C.K. (1991) 'Managing DMNCs: A search for a new paradigm', *Strategic Management Journal* 12: 145–164.

Duncan, R. and Weiss, A. (1979) 'Organizational learning: Implications for organizational design', in B. Staw (ed.) *Research in Organizational Behavior*, Greenwich, CT: JAI Press.

Dwyer, F.R., Schurr, P.H., and Oh, S. (1987) 'Developing buyer–seller relationships', *Journal of Marketing* 51 (April): 11–27.

Emerson, R.M. (1962) 'Power dependence relationships', *American Sociological Review* 27 (February): 31–41.

Festinger, L. (1957) *A Theory of Cognitive Dissonance*, Stanford, CA: Stanford University Press.

Fichman, M. and Levinthal, D.A. (1991) 'Honeymoons and the liability of adolescence: A new perspective on duration dependence in social and organizational relationships', *Academy of Management Review* 16: 442–468.

Fiol, C.M. and Lyles, M.A. (1985) 'Organizational learning', *Academy of Management Review* 10: 803–813.

Florida, R. and Kenney, M. (1991) 'Transplanted organizations: The transfer of Japanese industrial organization to the US', *American Sociological Review* 56: 381–398.

Fornell, C., Lorange, P., and Roos, J. (1990) 'The cooperative venture formation process: A latent variable structural modeling approach', *Management Science* 36: 1246–1256.

Franko, L. (1971) *Joint Venture Survival in Multinational Companies*, New York: Praeger.

Friedlander, F. (1984) 'Patterns of individual and organization learning', in S. Srivastva, and Associates (eds) *The Executive Mind*, San Francisco: Jossey-Bass Publishers.

Fruin, W.M. (1992) *The Japanese Enterprise System: Competitive Strategies and Cooperative Structures*, Oxford: Clarendon Press.

Geringer, J.M. and Hebert, L. (1989) 'Control and performance of international JVs', *Journal of International Business Studies* 20: 235–254.

—— (1991) 'Measuring performance of international joint ventures', *Journal of International Business Studies* 22: 253–267.

Gerlach, M.L. (1992a) 'The Japanese corporate network: A blockmodel analysis', *Administrative Science Quarterly* 37: 105–139.

—— (1992b) *Alliance Capitalism: The Social Organization of Japanese Business*, Berkeley: University of California Press.

Ghemawat, P. (1991) *Commitment: The Dynamic of Strategy*, New York: Free Press.

Ghoshal, S. (1987) 'Global strategy: An organizing framework', *Strategic Management Journal* 8: 425–440.

Gioia, D.A. and Manz, C.C. (1985) 'Linking cognition and behavior: A script processing interpretation of vicarious learning', *Academy of Management Review* 10: 527–539.

Glaser, B. (1978). *Theoretical Sensitivity*, Mill Valley, CA: Sociology Press.

Glaser, B.G. and Strauss, A.L. (1967) *The Discovery of Grounded Theory: Strategies for Qualitative Research*, New York: Aldine.

Gomes-Casseres, B. (1987) 'Joint venture instability: Is it a problem?', *Columbia Journal of World Business* 22 (Summer): 97–102.

Grant, R.M. (1991) 'The resource-based theory of competitive advantage: Implications for strategy formulation', California Management Review 33, 3: 119–135.

Gronhaug, K. (1977). 'Water to Spain: An export decision analyzed in the context of organization learning', *Journal of Management Studies* 14: 26–33.

Gupta, A.K. (1987) 'SBU strategies, corporate-SBU relations, and SBU effectiveness in strategy implementation', *Academy of Management Journal* 30: 477–500.

Hall, R.H., Clark, J.P., Giordano, P.C., Johnson, P.V., and Van Roekel, M. (1977) 'Patterns of interorganizational relationships', *Administrative Science Quarterly* 27: 457–474.

Hamada, T. (1991) *American Enterprise in Japan*, Albany: State University of New York Press.

Hamel, G. (1991) 'Competition for competence and inter-partner learning within international strategic alliances', *Strategic Management Journal* 12 (Special Issue): 83–104.

Hamel, G., Doz, Yves L., and Prahalad, C.K. (1989) 'Collaborate with your competitors – and win', *Harvard Business Review* 67, 1: 133–139.

Harrigan, K.R. (1985) *Strategies for Joint Ventures*, Lexington, MA: Lexington Books.

—— (1986) *Managing for JV Success*, Lexington, MA: Lexington Books.

Harrigan, K.R. and Newman, W. (1990) 'Bases of interorganizational co-operation: Propensity, power, persistence', *Journal of Management Studies* 27: 417–434.

Hedberg, B. (1981) 'How organizations learn and unlearn', in P. Nystrom and W. Starbuck (eds) *Handbook of Organizational Design*, London: Oxford University Press.

Hedlund, G. and Nonaka, I. (1993) 'Models of knowledge management in the west and Japan', in P. Lorange, B. Chakravarthy, J. Roos, and A. Van de Ven (eds) *Implementing Strategic Processes: Change, Learning, and Co-Operation*, Oxford: Basil Blackwell.

Heide, J.B. and Miner, A.S. (1992) 'The shadow of the future: Effects of anticipated interaction and frequency of contact on buyer–seller co-operation', *Academy of Management Journal* 35: 265–291.

Hennart, J.F. (1988) 'A transactions costs theory of equity JVs', *Strategic Management Journal* 9: 361–374.

—— (1991) 'The transactions cost theory of JVs: An empirical study of Japanese subsidiaries in the United States', *Management Science* 37: 483–497.

Hofer, C.W. and Schendel, D. (1986) *Strategy Formulation: Analytic Concepts*, St Paul, MN: West.

Horaguchi, H. (1991) *Japanese Overseas Investment*, Tokyo: University of Tokyo Press.

Huber, G.P. (1991) 'Organizational learning: The contributing processes and a review of the literatures', *Organization Science* 2: 88–117.

Huber, G.P. and Power, D.J. (1985) 'Retrospective reports of strategic-level managers: Guidelines for increasing their accuracy', *Strategic Management Journal* 6: 171–180.

Jacobson, G. and Hillkirk, J. (1986) *Xerox: American Samurai*, New York: Macmillan.

Jarillo, J.C. (1988) 'On strategic networks', *Strategic Management Journal* 9: 31–41.

Jelinek, M. (1979) *Institutionalizing Innovations: A Study of Organizational Learning Systems*, New York: Praeger.

Kahalas, H. and Suchon, K. (1992) 'Interview with Harold A. Poling, Chairman, CEO, Ford Motor Company', *Academy of Management Executive* 6, 2: 71–82.

Kanter, R.M. (1989) *When Giants Learn to Dance*, New York: Simon and Schuster.

Kearns, R.L. (1992) *Zaibatsu America: How Japanese Firms are Colonizing Vital US Industries*, New York: Free Press.

Keller, M. (1989) *Rude Awakening: The Rise, Fall, and Struggle for Recovery of General Motors*, New York: William Morrow.

Kester, W.C. (1991) *Japanese Takeovers: The Global Contest for Corporate Control*, Boston: Harvard Business School Press.

Keys, J.B., Denton, L.T., and Miller, T.R. (1994). 'The Japanese management theory jungle revisited', *Journal of Management* 20: 373–402.

Killing, J.P. (1982) 'How to make a global joint venture work', *Harvard Business Review* 3: 120–127.

—— (1983) *Strategies for JV Success*, New York: Praeger.

Kogut, B. (1988) 'JVs: Theoretical and empirical perspectives', *Strategic Management Journal* 9: 319–322.

—— (1989) 'The stability of joint ventures: Reciprocity and competitive rivalry', *The Journal of Industrial Economics* 38: 183–198.

Kogut, B. and Zander, U. (1992) 'Knowledge of the firm, combinative capabilities, and the replication of technology', *Organization Science* 3: 383–397.

Lawrence, P. and Lorsch, J. (1967) *Organization and Environment: Managing Differentiation and Environment*, Boston: Division of Research, Harvard Business School.

Lee, A.S. (1991) 'Integrating positivist and interpretive approaches to organizational research', *Organization Science* 4: 342–365.

Lenz, R.T. and Engledow, J.L. (1986) 'Environmental analysis: The applicability of current theory', *Strategic Management Journal* 7: 329–346.

Levinthal, D.A. (1991) 'Organizational adaptation and environmental selection – interrelated processes of change', *Organization Science* 2: 140–145.

Levinthal, D.A. and March, J.G. (1993) 'The myopia of learning', *Strategic Management Journal* 14: 95–112.

Levitt, B. and March, J.G. (1988) 'Organizational learning', *Annual Review of Sociology* 14: 319–340.

Lyles, M.A. (1988) 'Learning among JV-sophisticated firms', in F. Contractor and P. Lorange (eds) *Cooperative Strategies in International Business*, Toronto: Lexington Books.

McGee, J. and Thomas, H. (1986) 'Strategic groups: Theory, research and taxonomy', *Strategic Management Journal* 7: 141–160.

Mahoney, J.T. and Pandian, J.R. (1992) 'The resource-based view within the conversation of strategic management', *Strategic Management Journal* 13: 363–380.

March, J.G. (1991) 'Exploration and exploitation in organizational learning', *Organization Science* 2: 71–87.

March, J.G., Sproull, L.S., and Tamuz, M. (1991) 'Learning from samples of one or fewer', *Organization Science* 2: 1–13.

Mazur, J.E. (1990) *Learning and Behavior*, Englewood Cliffs, NJ: Prentice Hall.

Miles, M.B. and Huberman, A.M. (1984) *Qualitative Data Analysis: A Sourcebook of New Methods*, Newbury Park, CA: Sage.

Miles, R.E., and Snow, C.C. (1978) *Organizational Strategy, Structure and Process*, New York: McGraw Hill.

Miller, D. (1993) 'The architecture of simplicity', *Academy of Management Review* 18: 116–138.

Miller, E.K. and Winter, D. (1991) 'The other Big 3 are becoming all-American', *Ward's Auto World* 27, 2: 24–31.

Mintzberg, H. (1990) 'Strategy formation: Schools of thought', in J. Frederickson (ed.) *Perspectives of Strategic Management*, New York: Harper Business.

Neisser, U. (1976) *Cognition and Reality*, San Francisco: W.H. Freeman and Company.

Nelson, R.R. (1991) 'Why do firms differ, and how does it matter?', *Strategic Management Journal* 12 (Special Issue, Winter): 61–74.

Nelson, R.R. and Winter, Sidney G. (1982) *An Evolutionary Theory of Economic Change*, Cambridge, MA: Harvard University Press.

Nonaka, I. (1990) 'Redundant, overlapping organizations: A Japanese approach to managing the innovation process', *California Management Review* 32, 3: 27–38.

—— (1994) 'A dynamic theory of organizational knowledge', *Organization Science* 5: 14–37.

Nonaka, I. and Johansson, J.K. (1985) 'Organizational learning in Japanese companies', in R. Lamb and P. Shrivastava (eds) *Advances in Strategic Management*, volume 3, Greenwich, CT: JAI Press.

Odaka, K., Ono, K., and Adachi, F. (1988) *The Automobile Industry in Japan: A Study of Ancillary Firm Development*, Tokyo: Kinokuniya.

Ono, Y. (1991) 'Borden's breakup with Meiji Milk shows how a Japanese partnership can curdle', *Wall Street Journal*, 21 February: B1, B6.

Parkhe, A. (1991) 'Interfirm diversity, organizational learning, and longevity in global strategic alliances', *Journal of International Business Studies* 22: 579–602.

—— (1993) '"Messy" research, methodological predispositions, and theory development in international JVs', *Academy of Management Review* 18: 227–268.

Patton, M.Q. (1987) *How to Use Qualitative Methods in Evaluation*, Newbury Park, CA: Sage.

Pfeffer, J. and Salancik, G. R. (1978) *The External Control of Organizations: A Resource Dependence Perspective*, New York: Harper and Row.

Pinder, C.C. and Moore, L.F. (1980) 'The inevitability of multiple paradigms and the resultant need for middle-range analysis in organizational theory', in

C. Pinder and L. Moore (eds) *Middle Range Theory and the Study of Organizations*, Boston: Martinus Nijhof.

Porter, M.E. (1980) *Competitive Strategy*, New York: Free Press.

—— (1985) *Competitive Advantage*, New York: Free Press.

—— (1990) *The Competitive Advantage of Nations*, New York: Free Press.

—— (1991) 'Towards a dynamic theory of strategy', *Strategic Management Journal* 12 (Special Issue, Winter): 95–117.

Porter, M.E. and Fuller, M.B. (1986) 'Coalitions and global strategy', in M. Porter (ed.) *Competition in Global Industries*, Boston: Harvard Business School Press.

Powell, W.W. (1987) 'Hybrid organizational arrangements', *California Management Review* 30, 1: 67–87.

Prahalad, C.K. and Bettis, R.A. (1986) 'The dominant logic: A new linkage between diversity and performance', *Strategic Management Journal* 7: 485–501.

Prahalad, C.K. and Hamel, G. (1990) 'The core competence of the corporation', *Harvard Business Review* 68, 3: 79–91.

Prowse, S.B. (1992) 'The structure of corporate ownership in Japan', *Journal of Finance* 47: 1121–1140.

Pucik, V. (1991) 'Technology transfer in strategic alliances: Competitive collaboration and organizational learning', in T. Agmon and M. Von Glinow (eds) *Technology Transfer in International Business*, New York: Oxford University Press.

Reed, R. and DeFillippi, R.J. (1990) 'Causal ambiguity, barriers to imitation, and sustainable competitive advantage', *Academy of Management Review* 15: 88–102.

Reich, R. and Mankin, E. (1986) 'Joint ventures with Japan give away our future', *Harvard Business Review* 54, 2: 78–86.

Root, F. (1988) 'Some taxonomies of international cooperative arrangements', in F. Contractor and P. Lorange (eds) *Cooperative Strategies in International Business*, Toronto: Lexington Books.

Rumelt, R.P., Schendel, D., and Teece, D.J. (1991) 'Strategic management and economics', *Strategic Management Journal* 12 (Special Issue, Winter): 5–29.

Schaan, J.L. (1983) *Parent Control and JV Success: The Case of Mexico*, unpublished Ph.D. diss., University of Western Ontario.

Schein, E.H. (1971) *Coercive Persuasion*, New York: W.H. Norton and Co.

Schmidt, S.M. and Kochan, T.A. (1977) 'Interorganizational relationships: Patterns and motivations', *Administrative Science Quarterly* 22: 220–234.

Schwenk, C.R. and Dalton, D.R. (1991) 'The changing shape of strategic management research', *Advances in Strategic Management* 7: 277–300.

Shan, W. (1990) 'An empirical analysis of organizational strategies by entrepreneurial high-technology firms', *Strategic Management Journal* 11: 129–139.

Shortell, S.M. and Zajac, E.J. (1988) 'Internal corporate JVs: Development processes and performance outcomes', *Strategic Management Journal* 9: 527–542.

Shrivastava, P. (1986) 'Learning structures for top management', *Human Systems Management* 6: 35–44.

Shrivastava, P. and Schneider, S. (1986) 'Organizational frames of reference', *Human Relations* 37: 795–809.

Simonin, B.L. and Helleloid, D. (1993) 'Do organizations learn? An empirical test of organizational learning in international strategic alliances', in D. Moore (ed.) *Academy of Management Best Paper Proceedings 1993.*

Smith, D.C. (1989) 'Whatever happened to teamwork?', *Ward's Auto World* 25, 7: 3–44.

Smitka, M.J. (1991) *Competitive Ties in the Japanese Automotive Industry,* New York: Columbia University Press.

Starbuck, W.H. (1983) 'Organizations as action creators', *American Sociological Review* 48: 91–102.

—— (1992) 'Learning by knowledge intensive firms', *Journal of Management Studies* 29: 713–740.

Stinchcombe, A.L. (1965) 'Organizations and social structure', in J. March (ed.) *Handbook of Organizations,* Chicago: Rand-McNally.

Stopford, J.M. and Wells, L.T. (1972) *Managing the Multinational Enterprise,* New York: Basic Books.

Sullivan, J.J. (1992) 'Japanese management philosophies: From the vacuous to the brilliant', *California Management Review* 35 (Winter): 66–87.

Sullivan, J.J. and Peterson, R.B. (1982) 'Factors associated with trust in Japanese–American JVs', *Management International Review* 22, 2: 30–40.

Teece, D. (1982) 'Towards an economic theory of the multiproduct firm', *Journal of Economic Behavior and Organization* 3: 39–64.

—— (1984) 'Economic analysis and strategic management', *California Management Review* 26, 3: 87–110.

Thompson, J.D. (1967) *Organizations in Action,* New York: McGraw Hill.

Thorelli, H.B. (1986) 'Networks: Between markets and hierarchies', *Strategic Management Journal* 7: 37–51.

Turnbull, P.J. (1989) 'Industrial restructuring and labour relations in the automotive components industry: "Just-in-time" or "Just-too-late"?', in S. Tailby and C. Whitson (eds) *Manufacturing Change,* New York: Blackwell.

Turnbull, P.J., Oliver, N. and Wilkinson, B. (1992) 'Buyer–supplier relations in the UK automotive industry: Strategic implications of the Japanese manufacturing model', *Strategic Management Journal* 13: 159–168.

Turpin, D. (1993) 'Strategic alliances with Japanese firms: Myths and realities', *Long Range Planning* 26, 5: 11–16.

Tushman, M. (1977) 'Special roles in the innovation process', *Administrative Science Quarterly* 22: 587–605.

Tushman, M. and Scanlon, T.J. (1981) 'Boundary-scanning individuals: Their role in information transfer and their antecedents', *Academy of Management Journal* 24: 289–305.

Van de Ven, A.H. (1992) 'Suggestions for studying strategy process: A research note', *Strategic Management Journal* (Special Issue) 13: 169–188.

Walsh, J.P. and Ungson, G.R. (1991) 'Organizational memory', *Academy of Management Journal,* 16: 57–91.

Weick, K.E. (1979) *The Social Psychology of Organizing,* second edition [first edition 1969], Reading, MA: Addison-Wesley.

Westney, D.E. (1988) 'Domestic and foreign learning curves in managing international cooperative strategies', in F. Contractor and P. Lorange (eds) *Cooperative Strategies in International Business*, Toronto: Lexington Books.

Winter, S.G. (1986) 'The research program of the behavioral theory of the firm: Orthodox critique and evolutionary perspective', in B. Gilad and S. Kaish (eds) *Handbook of Behavioral Economics 1*, Greenwich, CT: JAI Press.

—— (1987) 'Knowledge and competence as strategic assets', in D. Teece (ed.) *The Competitive Challenge: Strategies for Industrial Innovation and Renewal*, Cambridge, MA.: Ballinger.

—— (1990) 'Survival, selection, and inheritance in evolutionary theories of organization', in J. Singh (ed.) *Organizational Evolution: New Directions*, Newbury Park, CA: Sage.

Womack, J.P. (1988) 'Multinational JVs in motor vehicles', in D. Mowery (ed.) *International Collaborative Ventures in US Manufacturing*, Cambridge, MA: Ballinger.

Yan, A. and Gray, G. (1994) 'Bargaining power, management control, and performance in United States–China joint ventures: A comparative case study', *Academy of Management Journal* 37: 1478–1517.

Yoshida, K. (1992) 'New economic principles in America – competition and cooperation: A comparative study of the US and Japan', *Columbia Journal of World Business* 26 (Winter): 30–44.

Zand, D.E. (1972) 'Trust and managerial problem solving', *Administrative Science Quarterly* 17: 229–239.

Index